Victor Hugo

Les Misérables - Volume II - Cosette

Book First - Waterloo

GRIN Verlag

Bibliografische Information der Deutschen Nationalbibliothek:

Die Deutsche Bibliothek verzeichnet diese Publikation in der Deutschen National-
bibliografie; detaillierte bibliografische Daten sind im Internet über http://dnb.d-
nb.de/ abrufbar.

Imprint:

Copyright © 2009 GRIN Verlag GmbH
Druck und Bindung: Books on Demand GmbH, Norderstedt Germany
ISBN: 978-3-640-24947-3

This book at GRIN:

http://www.grin.com/en/e-book/121208/les-miserables-volume-ii-cosette

GRIN - Your knowledge has value

Der GRIN Verlag publiziert seit 1998 wissenschaftliche Arbeiten von Studenten, Hochschullehrern und anderen Akademikern als eBook und gedrucktes Buch. Die Verlagswebsite www.grin.com ist die ideale Plattform zur Veröffentlichung von Hausarbeiten, Abschlussarbeiten, wissenschaftlichen Aufsätzen, Dissertationen und Fachbüchern.

Visit us on the internet:

http://www.grin.com/

http://www.facebook.com/grincom

http://www.twitter.com/grin_com

Victor Hugo

Les Misérables

Volume II

Cosette

BOOK FIRST - WATERLOO

[published 1887]

Summary

BOOK FIRST. WATERLOO

CHAPTER I. WHAT IS MET WITH ON THE WAY FROM NIVELLES

Last year (1861), on a beautiful May morning, a traveller, the person who is telling this story, was coming from Nivelles, and directing his course towards La Hulpe. He was on foot. He was pursuing a broad paved road, which undulated between two rows of trees, over the hills which succeed each other, raise the road and let it fall again, and produce something in the nature of enormous waves.

He had passed Lillois and Bois-Seigneur-Isaac. In the west he perceived the slate-roofed tower of Braine-l'Alleud, which has the form of a reversed vase. He had just left behind a wood upon an eminence; and at the angle of the cross-road, by the side of a sort of mouldy gibbet bearing the inscription Ancient Barrier No. 4, a public house, bearing on its front this sign: At the Four Winds (Aux Quatre Vents). Echabeau, Private Cafe.

A quarter of a league further on, he arrived at the bottom of a little valley, where there is water which passes beneath an arch made through the embankment of the road. The clump of sparsely planted but very green trees, which fills the valley on one side of the road, is dispersed over the meadows on the other, and disappears gracefully and as in order in the direction of Braine-l'Alleud.

On the right, close to the road, was an inn, with a four-wheeled cart at the door, a large bundle of hop-poles, a plough, a heap of dried brushwood near a flourishing hedge, lime smoking in a square hole, and a ladder suspended along an old penthouse with straw partitions. A young girl was weeding in a field, where a huge yellow poster, probably of some outside spectacle, such as a parish festival, was fluttering in the wind. At one corner of the inn, beside a pool in which a flotilla of ducks was navigating, a badly paved path plunged into the bushes. The wayfarer struck into this.

After traversing a hundred paces, skirting a wall of the fifteenth century, surmounted by a pointed gable, with bricks set in contrast, he found himself before a large door of arched stone, with a rectilinear impost, in the sombre style of Louis XIV., flanked by two flat medallions. A severe facade rose above this door; a wall, perpendicular to the facade, almost touched the door, and flanked it with an abrupt right angle. In the meadow before the door lay three harrows, through which, in disorder, grew all the flowers of May. The door was closed. The two decrepit leaves which barred it were ornamented with an old rusty knocker.

The sun was charming; the branches had that soft shivering of May, which seems to proceed rather from the nests than from the wind. A brave little bird, probably a lover, was carolling in a distracted manner in a large tree.

The wayfarer bent over and examined a rather large circular excavation, resembling the hollow of a sphere, in the stone on the left, at the foot of the pier of the door.

At this moment the leaves of the door parted, and a peasant woman emerged.

She saw the wayfarer, and perceived what he was looking at.

"It was a French cannon-ball which made that," she said to him. And she added:--

"That which you see there, higher up in the door, near a nail, is the hole of a big iron bullet as large as an egg. The bullet did not pierce the wood."

"What is the name of this place?" inquired the wayfarer.

"Hougomont," said the peasant woman.

The traveller straightened himself up. He walked on a few paces, and went off to look over the tops of the hedges. On the horizon through the trees, he perceived a sort of little elevation, and on this elevation something which at that distance resembled a lion.

He was on the battle-field of Waterloo.

CHAPTER II. HOUGOMONT

Hougomont,--this was a funereal spot, the beginning of the obstacle, the first resistance, which that great wood-cutter of Europe, called Napoleon, encountered at Waterloo, the first knot under the blows of his axe.

It was a chateau; it is no longer anything but a farm. For the antiquary, Hougomont is Hugomons. This manor was built by Hugo, Sire of Somerel, the same who endowed the sixth chaplaincy of the Abbey of Villiers.

The traveller pushed open the door, elbowed an ancient calash under the porch, and entered the courtyard.

The first thing which struck him in this paddock was a door of the sixteenth century, which here simulates an arcade, everything else having fallen prostrate around it. A monumental aspect often has its birth in ruin. In a wall near the arcade opens another arched door, of the time of Henry IV., permitting a glimpse of the trees of an orchard; beside this door, a manure-hole, some pickaxes, some shovels, some carts, an old well, with its flagstone and its iron reel, a chicken jumping, and a turkey spreading its tail, a chapel surmounted by a small bell-tower, a blossoming pear-tree trained in espalier against the wall of the chapel--behold the court, the conquest of which was one of Napoleon's dreams. This corner of earth, could he but have seized it, would, perhaps, have given him the world likewise. Chickens are scattering its dust abroad with their beaks. A growl is audible; it is a huge dog, who shows his teeth and replaces the English.

The English behaved admirably there. Cooke's four companies of guards there held out for seven hours against the fury of an army.

Hougomont viewed on the map, as a geometrical plan, comprising buildings and enclosures, presents a sort of irregular rectangle, one angle of which is nicked out. It is this angle which contains the southern door, guarded by this wall, which commands it only a gun's length away. Hougomont has two doors,--the southern door, that of the chateau; and the northern door, belonging to the farm. Napoleon sent his brother Jerome against Hougomont; the divisions of Foy, Guilleminot, and Bachelu hurled themselves against it; nearly the entire corps of Reille was employed against it, and miscarried; Kellermann's balls were exhausted on this heroic section of wall. Bauduin's brigade was not strong enough to force Hougomont on the north, and the brigade of Soye could not do more than effect the beginning of a breach on the south, but without taking it.

The farm buildings border the courtyard on the south. A bit of the north door, broken by the French, hangs suspended to the wall. It consists of four planks nailed to two cross-beams, on which the scars of the attack are visible.

The northern door, which was beaten in by the French, and which has had a piece applied to it to replace the panel suspended on the wall, stands half-open at the bottom of the paddock; it is cut squarely in the wall, built of stone below, of brick above which closes in the courtyard on the north. It is a simple door for carts, such as exist in all farms, with the two large leaves made of rustic planks: beyond lie the meadows. The dispute over this entrance was furious. For a long time, all sorts of imprints of bloody hands were visible on the door-posts. It was there that Bauduin was killed.

The storm of the combat still lingers in this courtyard; its horror is visible there; the confusion of the fray was petrified there; it lives and it dies there; it was only yesterday. The walls are in the death agony, the stones fall; the breaches cry aloud; the holes are wounds; the drooping, quivering trees seem to be making an effort to flee.

This courtyard was more built up in 1815 than it is to-day. Buildings which have since been pulled down then formed redans and angles.

The English barricaded themselves there; the French made their way in, but could not stand their ground. Beside the chapel, one wing of the chateau, the only ruin now remaining of the manor of Hougomont, rises in a crumbling state,--disembowelled, one might say. The chateau served for a dungeon, the chapel for a block-house. There men exterminated each other. The French, fired on from every point,--from behind the walls, from the summits of the garrets, from the depths of the cellars, through all the casements, through all the air-holes, through every crack in the stones,-- fetched fagots and set fire to walls and men; the reply to the grape-shot was a conflagration.

In the ruined wing, through windows garnished with bars of iron, the dismantled chambers of the main building of brick are visible; the English guards were in ambush in these rooms; the spiral of the staircase, cracked from the ground floor to the very roof, appears like the inside of a broken shell. The staircase has two stories; the English, besieged on the staircase, and massed on its upper steps, had cut off the lower steps. These consisted of large slabs of blue stone, which form a heap among the nettles. Half a score of steps still cling to the wall; on the first is cut the figure of a trident. These inaccessible steps are solid in their niches. All the rest resembles a jaw which has been denuded of its teeth. There are two old trees there: one is dead; the other is wounded at its base, and is clothed with verdure in April. Since 1815 it has taken to growing through the staircase.

A massacre took place in the chapel. The interior, which has recovered its calm, is singular. The mass has not been said there since the carnage. Nevertheless, the altar has been left there-- an altar of unpolished wood, placed against a background of roughhewn stone. Four whitewashed walls, a door opposite the altar, two small arched windows; over the door a large wooden crucifix, below the crucifix a square air-hole stopped up with a bundle of hay; on the ground, in one corner, an old window-frame with the glass all broken to pieces--such is the chapel. Near the altar there is nailed up a wooden statue of Saint Anne, of the fifteenth century; the head of the infant Jesus has been carried off by a large ball. The French, who were masters of the chapel for a moment, and were then dislodged, set fire to it. The flames filled this building; it was a perfect furnace; the door was burned, the floor was burned, the wooden Christ was not burned.

The fire preyed upon his feet, of which only the blackened stumps are now to be seen; then it stopped,-- a miracle, according to the assertion of the people of the neighborhood. The infant Jesus, decapitated, was less fortunate than the Christ.

The walls are covered with inscriptions. Near the feet of Christ this name is to be read: Henquinez. Then these others: Conde de Rio Maior Marques y Marquesa de Almagro (Habana). There are French names with exclamation points,--a sign of wrath. The wall was freshly whitewashed in 1849. The nations insulted each other there.

It was at the door of this chapel that the corpse was picked up which held an axe in its hand; this corpse was Sub-Lieutenant Legros.

On emerging from the chapel, a well is visible on the left. There are two in this courtyard. One inquires, Why is there no bucket and pulley to this? It is because water is no longer drawn there. Why is water not drawn there? Because it is full of skeletons.

The last person who drew water from the well was named Guillaume van Kylsom. He was a peasant who lived at Hougomont, and was gardener there. On the 18th of June, 1815, his family fled and concealed themselves in the woods.

The forest surrounding the Abbey of Villiers sheltered these unfortunate people who had been scattered abroad, for many days and nights. There are at this day certain traces recognizable, such as old boles of burned trees, which mark the site of these poor bivouacs trembling in the depths of the thickets.

Guillaume van Kylsom remained at Hougomont, "to guard the chateau," and concealed himself in the cellar. The English discovered him there. They tore him from his hiding-place, and the combatants forced this frightened man to serve them, by administering blows with the flats of their swords. They were thirsty; this Guillaume brought them water. It was from this well that he drew it. Many drank there their last draught. This well where drank so many of the dead was destined to die itself.

After the engagement, they were in haste to bury the dead bodies. Death has a fashion of harassing victory, and she causes the pest to follow glory. The typhus is a concomitant of triumph. This well was deep, and it was turned into a sepulchre. Three hundred dead bodies were cast into it. With too much haste perhaps. Were they all dead? Legend says they were not. It seems that on the night succeeding the interment, feeble voices were heard calling from the well.

This well is isolated in the middle of the courtyard. Three walls, part stone, part brick, and simulating a small, square tower, and folded like the leaves of a screen, surround it on all sides. The fourth side is open. It is there that the water was drawn. The wall at the bottom has a sort of shapeless loophole, possibly the hole made by a shell. This little tower had a platform, of which only the beams remain. The iron supports of the well on the right form a cross. On leaning over, the eye is lost in a deep cylinder of brick which is filled with a heaped-up mass of shadows. The base of the walls all about the well is concealed in a growth of nettles.

This well has not in front of it that large blue slab which forms the table for all wells in Belgium. The slab has here been replaced by a cross-beam, against which lean five or six shapeless fragments of knotty and petrified wood which resemble huge bones. There is no longer either pail, chain, or pulley; but there is still the stone basin which served the overflow. The rain-water collects there, and from time to time a bird of the neighboring forests comes thither to drink, and then flies away. One house in this ruin, the farmhouse, is still inhabited. The door of this house opens on the courtyard. Upon this door, beside a pretty Gothic lock-plate, there is an iron handle with trefoils placed slanting. At the moment when the Hanoverian lieutenant, Wilda, grasped this handle in order to take refuge in the farm, a French sapper hewed off his hand with an axe.

The family who occupy the house had for their grandfather Guillaume van Kylsom, the old gardener, dead long since. A woman with gray hair said to us: "I was there. I was three years old. My sister, who was older, was terrified and wept. They carried us off to the woods. I went there in my mother's arms. We glued our ears to the earth to hear. I imitated the cannon, and went boum! boum!"

A door opening from the courtyard on the left led into the orchard, so we were told. The orchard is terrible.

It is in three parts; one might almost say, in three acts. The first part is a garden, the second is an orchard, the third is a wood. These three parts have a common enclosure: on the side of the entrance, the buildings of the chateau and the farm; on the left, a hedge; on the right, a wall; and at the end, a wall. The wall on the right is of brick, the wall at the bottom is of stone. One enters the garden first. It slopes downwards, is planted with gooseberry bushes, choked with a wild growth of vegetation, and terminated by a monumental terrace of cut stone, with balustrade with a double curve.

It was a seignorial garden in the first French style which preceded Le Notre; to-day it is ruins and briars. The pilasters are surmounted by globes which resemble cannon-balls of stone. Forty-three balusters can still be counted on their sockets;

the rest lie prostrate in the grass. Almost all bear scratches of bullets. One broken baluster is placed on the pediment like a fractured leg.

It was in this garden, further down than the orchard, that six light-infantry men of the 1st, having made their way thither, and being unable to escape, hunted down and caught like bears in their dens, accepted the combat with two Hanoverian companies, one of which was armed with carbines. The Hanoverians lined this balustrade and fired from above. The infantry men, replying from below, six against two hundred, intrepid and with no shelter save the currant-bushes, took a quarter of an hour to die.

One mounts a few steps and passes from the garden into the orchard, properly speaking. There, within the limits of those few square fathoms, fifteen hundred men fell in less than an hour. The wall seems ready to renew the combat. Thirty-eight loopholes, pierced by the English at irregular heights, are there still. In front of the sixth are placed two English tombs of granite. There are loopholes only in the south wall, as the principal attack came from that quarter. The wall is hidden on the outside by a tall hedge; the French came up, thinking that they had to deal only with a hedge, crossed it, and found the wall both an obstacle and an ambuscade, with the English guards behind it, the thirty-eight loopholes firing at once a shower of grape-shot and balls, and Soye's brigade was broken against it. Thus Waterloo began.

Nevertheless, the orchard was taken. As they had no ladders, the French scaled it with their nails. They fought hand to hand amid the trees. All this grass has been soaked in blood. A battalion of Nassau, seven hundred strong, was overwhelmed there. The outside of the wall, against which Kellermann's two batteries were trained, is gnawed by grape-shot.

This orchard is sentient, like others, in the month of May. It has its buttercups and its daisies; the grass is tall there; the cart-horses browse there; cords of hair, on which linen is drying, traverse the spaces between the trees and force the passer-by to bend his head; one walks over this uncultivated land, and one's foot dives into mole-holes. In the middle of the grass one observes an uprooted tree-bole which lies there all verdant. Major Blackmann leaned against it to die. Beneath a great tree in the neighborhood fell the German general, Duplat, descended from a French family which fled on the revocation of the Edict of Nantes. An aged and falling apple-tree leans far over to one side, its wound dressed with a bandage of straw and of clayey loam. Nearly all the apple-trees are falling with age. There is not one which has not had its bullet or its biscayan.[1]

---

1   A bullet as large as an egg.

The skeletons of dead trees abound in this orchard. Crows fly through their branches, and at the end of it is a wood full of violets.

Bauduin, killed, Foy wounded, conflagration, massacre, carnage, a rivulet formed of English blood, French blood, German blood mingled in fury, a well crammed with corpses, the regiment of Nassau and the regiment of Brunswick destroyed, Duplat killed, Blackmann killed, the English Guards mutilated, twenty French battalions, besides the forty from Reille's corps, decimated, three thousand men in that hovel of Hougomont alone cut down, slashed to pieces, shot, burned, with their throats cut,--and all this so that a peasant can say to-day to the traveller: Monsieur, give me three francs, and if you like, I will explain to you the affair of Waterloo!

CHAPTER III. THE EIGHTEENTH OF JUNE, 1815

Let us turn back,--that is one of the story-teller's rights,-- and put ourselves once more in the year 1815, and even a little earlier than the epoch when the action narrated in the first part of this book took place.

If it had not rained in the night between the 17th and the 18th of June, 1815, the fate of Europe would have been different. A few drops of water, more or less, decided the downfall of Napoleon. All that Providence required in order to make Waterloo the end of Austerlitz was a little more rain, and a cloud traversing the sky out of season sufficed to make a world crumble.

The battle of Waterloo could not be begun until half-past eleven o'clock, and that gave Blucher time to come up. Why? Because the ground was wet. The artillery had to wait until it became a little firmer before they could manoeuvre.

Napoleon was an artillery officer, and felt the effects of this. The foundation of this wonderful captain was the man who, in the report to the Directory on Aboukir, said: Such a one of our balls killed six men. All his plans of battle were arranged for projectiles. The key to his victory was to make the artillery converge on one point. He treated the strategy of the hostile general like a citadel, and made a breach in it. He overwhelmed the weak point with grape-shot; he joined and dissolved battles with cannon. There was something of the sharpshooter in his genius. To beat in squares, to pulverize regiments, to break lines, to crush and disperse masses,--for him everything lay in this, to strike, strike, strike incessantly,-- and he intrusted this task to the cannon-ball. A redoubtable method, and one which, united with genius, rendered this gloomy athlete of the pugilism of war invincible for the space of fifteen years.

On the 18th of June, 1815, he relied all the more on his artillery, because he had numbers on his side. Wellington had only one hundred and fifty-nine mouths of fire; Napoleon had two hundred and forty.

Suppose the soil dry, and the artillery capable of moving, the action would have begun at six o'clock in the morning. The battle would have been won and ended at two o'clock, three hours before the change of fortune in favor of the Prussians. What amount of blame attaches to Napoleon for the loss of this battle? Is the shipwreck due to the pilot?

Was it the evident physical decline of Napoleon that complicated this epoch by an inward diminution of force? Had the twenty years of war worn out the blade as it had worn the scabbard, the soul as well as the body? Did the veteran make himself disastrously felt in the leader? In a word, was this genius, as many historians of note have thought, suffering from an eclipse? Did he go into a frenzy in order to disguise his weakened powers from himself? Did he begin to waver under the delusion of a breath of adventure? Had he become--a grave matter in a general--unconscious of peril? Is there an age, in this class of material great men, who may be called the giants of action, when genius grows short-sighted? Old age has no hold on the geniuses of the ideal; for the Dantes and Michael Angelos to grow old is to grow in greatness; is it to grow less for the Hannibals and the Bonapartes? Had Napoleon lost the direct sense of victory? Had he reached the point where he could no longer recognize the reef, could no longer divine the snare, no longer discern the crumbling brink of abysses? Had he lost his power of scenting out catastrophes? He who had in former days known all the roads to triumph, and who, from the summit of his chariot of lightning, pointed them out with a sovereign finger, had he now reached that state of sinister amazement when he could lead his tumultuous legions harnessed to it, to the precipice? Was he seized at the age of forty-six with a supreme madness? Was that titanic charioteer of destiny no longer anything more than an immense dare-devil?

We do not think so.

His plan of battle was, by the confession of all, a masterpiece. To go straight to the centre of the Allies' line, to make a breach in the enemy, to cut them in two, to drive the British half back on Hal, and the Prussian half on Tongres, to make two shattered fragments of Wellington and Blucher, to carry Mont-Saint-Jean, to seize Brussels, to hurl the German into the Rhine, and the Englishman into the sea. All this was contained in that battle, according to Napoleon. Afterwards people would see.

12

Of course, we do not here pretend to furnish a history of the battle of Waterloo; one of the scenes of the foundation of the story which we are relating is connected with this battle, but this history is not our subject; this history, moreover, has been finished, and finished in a masterly manner, from one point of view by Napoleon, and from another point of view by a whole pleiad of historians.[2]

As for us, we leave the historians at loggerheads; we are but a distant witness, a passer-by on the plain, a seeker bending over that soil all made of human flesh, taking appearances for realities, perchance; we have no right to oppose, in the name of science, a collection of facts which contain illusions, no doubt; we possess neither military practice nor strategic ability which authorize a system; in our opinion, a chain of accidents dominated the two leaders at Waterloo; and when it becomes a question of destiny, that mysterious culprit, we judge like that ingenious judge, the populace.

CHAPTER IV. A

Those persons who wish to gain a clear idea of the battle of Waterloo have only to place, mentally, on the ground, a capital A. The left limb of the A is the road to Nivelles, the right limb is the road to Genappe, the tie of the A is the hollow road to Ohain from Braine-l'Alleud. The top of the A is Mont-Saint-Jean, where Wellington is; the lower left tip is Hougomont, where Reille is stationed with Jerome Bonaparte; the right tip is the Belle-Alliance, where Napoleon was. At the centre of this chord is the precise point where the final word of the battle was pronounced. It was there that the lion has been placed, the involuntary symbol of the supreme heroism of the Imperial Guard.

The triangle included in the top of the A, between the two limbs and the tie, is the plateau of Mont-Saint-Jean. The dispute over this plateau constituted the whole battle. The wings of the two armies extended to the right and left of the two roads to Genappe and Nivelles; d'Erlon facing Picton, Reille facing Hill.

Behind the tip of the A, behind the plateau of Mont-Saint-Jean, is the forest of Soignes.

As for the plain itself, let the reader picture to himself a vast undulating sweep of ground; each rise commands the next rise, and all the undulations mount towards Mont-Saint-Jean, and there end in the forest.

---

2 Walter Scott, Lamartine, Vaulabelle, Charras, Quinet, Thiers.

Two hostile troops on a field of battle are two wrestlers. It is a question of seizing the opponent round the waist. The one seeks to trip up the other. They clutch at everything: a bush is a point of support; an angle of the wall offers them a rest to the shoulder; for the lack of a hovel under whose cover they can draw up, a regiment yields its ground; an unevenness in the ground, a chance turn in the landscape, a cross-path encountered at the right moment, a grove, a ravine, can stay the heel of that colossus which is called an army, and prevent its retreat. He who quits the field is beaten; hence the necessity devolving on the responsible leader, of examining the most insignificant clump of trees, and of studying deeply the slightest relief in the ground.

The two generals had attentively studied the plain of Mont-Saint-Jean, now called the plain of Waterloo. In the preceding year, Wellington, with the sagacity of foresight, had examined it as the possible seat of a great battle. Upon this spot, and for this duel, on the 18th of June, Wellington had the good post, Napoleon the bad post. The English army was stationed above, the French army below.

It is almost superfluous here to sketch the appearance of Napoleon on horseback, glass in hand, upon the heights of Rossomme, at daybreak, on June 18, 1815. All the world has seen him before we can show him. That calm profile under the little three-cornered hat of the school of Brienne, that green uniform, the white revers concealing the star of the Legion of Honor, his great coat hiding his epaulets, the corner of red ribbon peeping from beneath his vest, his leather trousers, the white horse with the saddle-cloth of purple velvet bearing on the corners crowned N's and eagles, Hessian boots over silk stockings, silver spurs, the sword of Marengo,--that whole figure of the last of the Caesars is present to all imaginations, saluted with acclamations by some, severely regarded by others.

That figure stood for a long time wholly in the light; this arose from a certain legendary dimness evolved by the majority of heroes, and which always veils the truth for a longer or shorter time; but to-day history and daylight have arrived.

That light called history is pitiless; it possesses this peculiar and divine quality, that, pure light as it is, and precisely because it is wholly light, it often casts a shadow in places where people had hitherto beheld rays; from the same man it constructs two different phantoms, and the one attacks the other and executes justice on it, and the shadows of the despot contend with the brilliancy of the leader. Hence arises a truer measure in the definitive judgments of nations. Babylon violated lessens Alexander, Rome enchained lessens Caesar, Jerusalem murdered lessens Titus, tyranny follows the tyrant. It is a misfortune for a man to leave behind him the night which bears his form.

CHAPTER V. THE QUID OBSCURUM OF BATTLES

Every one is acquainted with the first phase of this battle; a beginning which was troubled, uncertain, hesitating, menacing to both armies, but still more so for the English than for the French.

It had rained all night, the earth had been cut up by the downpour, the water had accumulated here and there in the hollows of the plain as if in casks; at some points the gear of the artillery carriages was buried up to the axles, the circingles of the horses were dripping with liquid mud. If the wheat and rye trampled down by this cohort of transports on the march had not filled in the ruts and strewn a litter beneath the wheels, all movement, particularly in the valleys, in the direction of Papelotte would have been impossible.

The affair began late. Napoleon, as we have already explained, was in the habit of keeping all his artillery well in hand, like a pistol, aiming it now at one point, now at another, of the battle; and it had been his wish to wait until the horse batteries could move and gallop freely. In order to do that it was necessary that the sun should come out and dry the soil. But the sun did not make its appearance. It was no longer the rendezvous of Austerlitz. When the first cannon was fired, the English general, Colville, looked at his watch, and noted that it was thirty-five minutes past eleven.

The action was begun furiously, with more fury, perhaps, than the Emperor would have wished, by the left wing of the French resting on Hougomont. At the same time Napoleon attacked the centre by hurling Quiot's brigade on La Haie-Sainte, and Ney pushed forward the right wing of the French against the left wing of the English, which rested on Papelotte.

The attack on Hougomont was something of a feint; the plan was to draw Wellington thither, and to make him swerve to the left. This plan would have succeeded if the four companies of the English guards and the brave Belgians of Perponcher's division had not held the position solidly, and Wellington, instead of massing his troops there, could confine himself to despatching thither, as reinforcements, only four more companies of guards and one battalion from Brunswick.

The attack of the right wing of the French on Papelotte was calculated, in fact, to overthrow the English left, to cut off the road to Brussels, to bar the passage against possible Prussians, to force Mont-Saint-Jean, to turn Wellington back on

15

Hougomont, thence on Braine-l'Alleud, thence on Hal; nothing easier. With the exception of a few incidents this attack succeeded Papelotte was taken; La Haie-Sainte was carried.

A detail to be noted. There was in the English infantry, particularly in Kempt's brigade, a great many raw recruits. These young soldiers were valiant in the presence of our redoubtable infantry; their inexperience extricated them intrepidly from the dilemma; they performed particularly excellent service as skirmishers: the soldier skirmisher, left somewhat to himself, becomes, so to speak, his own general. These recruits displayed some of the French ingenuity and fury. This novice of an infantry had dash. This displeased Wellington.

After the taking of La Haie-Sainte the battle wavered.

There is in this day an obscure interval, from mid-day to four o'clock; the middle portion of this battle is almost indistinct, and participates in the sombreness of the hand-to-hand conflict. Twilight reigns over it. We perceive vast fluctuations in that fog, a dizzy mirage, paraphernalia of war almost unknown to-day, pendant colbacks, floating sabre-taches, cross-belts, cartridge-boxes for grenades, hussar dolmans, red boots with a thousand wrinkles, heavy shakos garlanded with torsades, the almost black infantry of Brunswick mingled with the scarlet infantry of England, the English soldiers with great, white circular pads on the slopes of their shoulders for epaulets, the Hanoverian light-horse with their oblong casques of leather, with brass hands and red horse-tails, the Scotch with their bare knees and plaids, the great white gaiters of our grenadiers; pictures, not strategic lines--what Salvator Rosa requires, not what is suited to the needs of Gribeauval.

A certain amount of tempest is always mingled with a battle. Quid obscurum, quid divinum. Each historian traces, to some extent, the particular feature which pleases him amid this pell-mell. Whatever may be the combinations of the generals, the shock of armed masses has an incalculable ebb. During the action the plans of the two leaders enter into each other and become mutually thrown out of shape. Such a point of the field of battle devours more combatants than such another, just as more or less spongy soils soak up more or less quickly the water which is poured on them. It becomes necessary to pour out more soldiers than one would like; a series of expenditures which are the unforeseen. The line of battle waves and undulates like a thread, the trails of blood gush illogically, the fronts of the armies waver, the regiments form capes and gulfs as they enter and withdraw; all these reefs are continually moving in front of each other. Where the infantry stood the artillery arrives, the cavalry rushes in where the artillery was, the battalions are like smoke. There was something there; seek it. It

16

has disappeared; the open spots change place, the sombre folds advance and retreat, a sort of wind from the sepulchre pushes forward, hurls back, distends, and disperses these tragic multitudes. What is a fray? an oscillation? The immobility of a mathematical plan expresses a minute, not a day. In order to depict a battle, there is required one of those powerful painters who have chaos in their brushes. Rembrandt is better than Vandermeulen; Vandermeulen, exact at noon, lies at three o'clock. Geometry is deceptive; the hurricane alone is trustworthy. That is what confers on Folard the right to contradict Polybius. Let us add, that there is a certain instant when the battle degenerates into a combat, becomes specialized, and disperses into innumerable detailed feats, which, to borrow the expression of Napoleon himself, "belong rather to the biography of the regiments than to the history of the army." The historian has, in this case, the evident right to sum up the whole. He cannot do more than seize the principal outlines of the struggle, and it is not given to any one narrator, however conscientious he may be, to fix, absolutely, the form of that horrible cloud which is called a battle.

This, which is true of all great armed encounters, is particularly applicable to Waterloo.

Nevertheless, at a certain moment in the afternoon the battle came to a point.

CHAPTER VI. FOUR O'CLOCK IN THE AFTERNOON

Towards four o'clock the condition of the English army was serious. The Prince of Orange was in command of the centre, Hill of the right wing, Picton of the left wing. The Prince of Orange, desperate and intrepid, shouted to the Hollando-Belgians: "Nassau! Brunswick! Never retreat!" Hill, having been weakened, had come up to the support of Wellington; Picton was dead. At the very moment when the English had captured from the French the flag of the 105th of the line, the French had killed the English general, Picton, with a bullet through the head. The battle had, for Wellington, two bases of action, Hougomont and La Haie-Sainte; Hougomont still held out, but was on fire; La Haie-Sainte was taken. Of the German battalion which defended it, only forty-two men survived; all the officers, except five, were either dead or captured. Three thousand combatants had been massacred in that barn. A sergeant of the English Guards, the foremost boxer in England, reputed invulnerable by his companions, had been killed there by a little French drummer-boy. Baring had been dislodged, Alten put to the sword. Many flags had been lost, one from Alten's division, and one from the battalion of Lunenburg, carried by a prince of the house of Deux-Ponts. The Scotch Grays no longer existed; Ponsonby's great dragoons had been hacked to pieces. That valiant cavalry had bent beneath

17

the lancers of Bro and beneath the cuirassiers of Travers; out of twelve hundred horses, six hundred remained; out of three lieutenant-colonels, two lay on the earth,--Hamilton wounded, Mater slain. Ponsonby had fallen, riddled by seven lance-thrusts. Gordon was dead. Marsh was dead. Two divisions, the fifth and the sixth, had been annihilated.

Hougomont injured, La Haie-Sainte taken, there now existed but one rallying-point, the centre. That point still held firm. Wellington reinforced it. He summoned thither Hill, who was at Merle-Braine; he summoned Chasse, who was at Braine-l'Alleud.

The centre of the English army, rather concave, very dense, and very compact, was strongly posted. It occupied the plateau of Mont-Saint-Jean, having behind it the village, and in front of it the slope, which was tolerably steep then. It rested on that stout stone dwelling which at that time belonged to the domain of Nivelles, and which marks the intersection of the roads--a pile of the sixteenth century, and so robust that the cannon-balls rebounded from it without injuring it. All about the plateau the English had cut the hedges here and there, made embrasures in the hawthorn-trees, thrust the throat of a cannon between two branches, embattled the shrubs. There artillery was ambushed in the brushwood. This punic labor, incontestably authorized by war, which permits traps, was so well done, that Haxo, who had been despatched by the Emperor at nine o'clock in the morning to reconnoitre the enemy's batteries, had discovered nothing of it, and had returned and reported to Napoleon that there were no obstacles except the two barricades which barred the road to Nivelles and to Genappe. It was at the season when the grain is tall; on the edge of the plateau a battalion of Kempt's brigade, the 95th, armed with carabines, was concealed in the tall wheat.

Thus assured and buttressed, the centre of the Anglo-Dutch army was well posted. The peril of this position lay in the forest of Soignes, then adjoining the field of battle, and intersected by the ponds of Groenendael and Boitsfort. An army could not retreat thither without dissolving; the regiments would have broken up immediately there. The artillery would have been lost among the morasses. The retreat, according to many a man versed in the art,--though it is disputed by others,--would have been a disorganized flight.

To this centre, Wellington added one of Chasse's brigades taken from the right wing, and one of Wincke's brigades taken from the left wing, plus Clinton's division. To his English, to the regiments of Halkett, to the brigades of Mitchell, to the guards of Maitland, he gave as reinforcements and aids, the infantry of Brunswick, Nassau's contingent, Kielmansegg's Hanoverians, and Ompteda's

Germans. This placed twenty-six battalions under his hand. The right wing, as Charras says, was thrown back on the centre. An enormous battery was masked by sacks of earth at the spot where there now stands what is called the "Museum of Waterloo." Besides this, Wellington had, behind a rise in the ground, Somerset's Dragoon Guards, fourteen hundred horse strong. It was the remaining half of the justly celebrated English cavalry. Ponsonby destroyed, Somerset remained.

The battery, which, if completed, would have been almost a redoubt, was ranged behind a very low garden wall, backed up with a coating of bags of sand and a large slope of earth. This work was not finished; there had been no time to make a palisade for it.

Wellington, uneasy but impassive, was on horseback, and there remained the whole day in the same attitude, a little in advance of the old mill of Mont-Saint-Jean, which is still in existence, beneath an elm, which an Englishman, an enthusiastic vandal, purchased later on for two hundred francs, cut down, and carried off. Wellington was coldly heroic. The bullets rained about him. His aide-de-camp, Gordon, fell at his side. Lord Hill, pointing to a shell which had burst, said to him: "My lord, what are your orders in case you are killed?" "To do like me," replied Wellington. To Clinton he said laconically, "To hold this spot to the last man." The day was evidently turning out ill. Wellington shouted to his old companions of Talavera, of Vittoria, of Salamanca: "Boys, can retreat be thought of? Think of old England!"

Towards four o'clock, the English line drew back. Suddenly nothing was visible on the crest of the plateau except the artillery and the sharpshooters; the rest had disappeared: the regiments, dislodged by the shells and the French bullets, retreated into the bottom, now intersected by the back road of the farm of Mont-Saint-Jean; a retrograde movement took place, the English front hid itself, Wellington drew back. "The beginning of retreat!" cried Napoleon.

CHAPTER VII. NAPOLEON IN A GOOD HUMOR

The Emperor, though ill and discommoded on horseback by a local trouble, had never been in a better humor than on that day. His impenetrability had been smiling ever since the morning. On the 18th of June, that profound soul masked by marble beamed blindly. The man who had been gloomy at Austerlitz was gay at Waterloo. The greatest favorites of destiny make mistakes. Our joys are composed of shadow. The supreme smile is God's alone.

Ridet Caesar, Pompeius flebit, said the legionaries of the Fulminatrix Legion. Pompey was not destined to weep on that occasion, but it is certain that Caesar laughed. While exploring on horseback at one o'clock on the preceding night, in storm and rain, in company with Bertrand, the communes in the neighborhood of Rossomme, satisfied at the sight of the long line of the English camp-fires illuminating the whole horizon from Frischemont to Braine-l'Alleud, it had seemed to him that fate, to whom he had assigned a day on the field of Waterloo, was exact to the appointment; he stopped his horse, and remained for some time motionless, gazing at the lightning and listening to the thunder; and this fatalist was heard to cast into the darkness this mysterious saying, "We are in accord." Napoleon was mistaken. They were no longer in accord.

He took not a moment for sleep; every instant of that night was marked by a joy for him. He traversed the line of the principal outposts, halting here and there to talk to the sentinels. At half-past two, near the wood of Hougomont, he heard the tread of a column on the march; he thought at the moment that it was a retreat on the part of Wellington. He said: "It is the rear-guard of the English getting under way for the purpose of decamping. I will take prisoners the six thousand English who have just arrived at Ostend." He conversed expansively; he regained the animation which he had shown at his landing on the first of March, when he pointed out to the Grand-Marshal the enthusiastic peasant of the Gulf Juan, and cried, "Well, Bertrand, here is a reinforcement already!" On the night of the 17th to the 18th of June he rallied Wellington. "That little Englishman needs a lesson," said Napoleon. The rain redoubled in violence; the thunder rolled while the Emperor was speaking.

At half-past three o'clock in the morning, he lost one illusion; officers who had been despatched to reconnoitre announced to him that the enemy was not making any movement. Nothing was stirring; not a bivouac-fire had been extinguished; the English army was asleep. The silence on earth was profound; the only noise was in the heavens. At four o'clock, a peasant was brought in to him by the scouts; this peasant had served as guide to a brigade of English cavalry, probably Vivian's brigade, which was on its way to take up a position in the village of Ohain, at the extreme left. At five o'clock, two Belgian deserters reported to him that they had just quitted their regiment, and that the English army was ready for battle. "So much the better!" exclaimed Napoleon. "I prefer to overthrow them rather than to drive them back."

In the morning he dismounted in the mud on the slope which forms an angle with the Plancenoit road, had a kitchen table and a peasant's chair brought to him from the farm of Rossomme, seated himself, with a truss of straw for a carpet, and spread out on the table the chart of the battle-field, saying to Soult as he did so, "A pretty checker-board."

In consequence of the rains during the night, the transports of provisions, embedded in the soft roads, had not been able to arrive by morning; the soldiers had had no sleep; they were wet and fasting. This did not prevent Napoleon from exclaiming cheerfully to Ney, "We have ninety chances out of a hundred." At eight o'clock the Emperor's breakfast was brought to him. He invited many generals to it. During breakfast, it was said that Wellington had been to a ball two nights before, in Brussels, at the Duchess of Richmond's; and Soult, a rough man of war, with a face of an archbishop, said, "The ball takes place to-day." The Emperor jested with Ney, who said, "Wellington will not be so simple as to wait for Your Majesty." That was his way, however. "He was fond of jesting," says Fleury de Chaboulon. "A merry humor was at the foundation of his character," says Gourgaud. "He abounded in pleasantries, which were more peculiar than witty," says Benjamin Constant. These gayeties of a giant are worthy of insistence. It was he who called his grenadiers "his grumblers"; he pinched their ears; he pulled their mustaches. "The Emperor did nothing but play pranks on us," is the remark of one of them. During the mysterious trip from the island of Elba to France, on the 27th of February, on the open sea, the French brig of war, Le Zephyr, having encountered the brig L'Inconstant, on which Napoleon was concealed, and having asked the news of Napoleon from L'Inconstant, the Emperor, who still wore in his hat the white and amaranthine cockade sown with bees, which he had adopted at the isle of Elba, laughingly seized the speaking-trumpet, and answered for himself, "The Emperor is well." A man who laughs like that is on familiar terms with events. Napoleon indulged in many fits of this laughter during the breakfast at Waterloo. After breakfast he meditated for a quarter of an hour; then two generals seated themselves on the truss of straw, pen in hand and their paper on their knees, and the Emperor dictated to them the order of battle.

At nine o'clock, at the instant when the French army, ranged in echelons and set in motion in five columns, had deployed-- the divisions in two lines, the artillery between the brigades, the music at their head; as they beat the march, with rolls on the drums and the blasts of trumpets, mighty, vast, joyous, a sea of casques, of sabres, and of bayonets on the horizon, the Emperor was touched, and twice exclaimed, "Magnificent! Magnificent!"

Between nine o'clock and half-past ten the whole army, incredible as it may appear, had taken up its position and ranged itself in six lines, forming, to repeat the Emperor's expression, "the figure of six V's." A few moments after the formation of the battle-array, in the midst of that profound silence, like that which heralds the beginning of a storm, which precedes engagements, the Emperor tapped Haxo on the shoulder, as he beheld the three batteries of twelve-pounders, detached by his orders from the corps of Erlon, Reille, and Lobau, and destined to begin the action by taking Mont-Saint-Jean, which was situated at the intersection of the Nivelles and the Genappe roads, and said to him, "There are four and twenty handsome maids, General."

Sure of the issue, he encouraged with a smile, as they passed before him, the company of sappers of the first corps, which he had appointed to barricade Mont-Saint-Jean as soon as the village should be carried. All this serenity had been traversed by but a single word of haughty pity; perceiving on his left, at a spot where there now stands a large tomb, those admirable Scotch Grays, with their superb horses, massing themselves, he said, "It is a pity."

Then he mounted his horse, advanced beyond Rossomme, and selected for his post of observation a contracted elevation of turf to the right of the road from Genappe to Brussels, which was his second station during the battle. The third station, the one adopted at seven o'clock in the evening, between La Belle-Alliance and La Haie-Sainte, is formidable; it is a rather elevated knoll, which still exists, and behind which the guard was massed on a slope of the plain. Around this knoll the balls rebounded from the pavements of the road, up to Napoleon himself. As at Brienne, he had over his head the shriek of the bullets and of the heavy artillery. Mouldy cannon-balls, old sword-blades, and shapeless projectiles, eaten up with rust, were picked up at the spot where his horse' feet stood. Scabra rubigine. A few years ago, a shell of sixty pounds, still charged, and with its fuse broken off level with the bomb, was unearthed. It was at this last post that the Emperor said to his guide, Lacoste, a hostile and terrified peasant, who was attached to the saddle of a hussar, and who turned round at every discharge of canister and tried to hide behind Napoleon: "Fool, it is shameful! You'll get yourself killed with a ball in the back." He who writes these lines has himself found, in the friable soil of this knoll, on turning over the sand, the remains of the neck of a bomb, disintegrated, by the oxidization of six and forty years, and old fragments of iron which parted like elder-twigs between the fingers.

Every one is aware that the variously inclined undulations of the plains, where the engagement between Napoleon and Wellington took place, are no longer what they were on June 18, 1815. By taking from this mournful field the wherewithal to make a monument to it, its real relief has been taken away, and history, disconcerted, no longer finds her bearings there. It has been disfigured for the sake of glorifying it. Wellington, when he beheld Waterloo once more, two years later, exclaimed, "They have altered my field of battle!" Where the great pyramid of earth, surmounted by the lion, rises to-day, there was a hillock which descended in an easy slope towards the Nivelles road, but which was almost an escarpment on the side of the highway to Genappe. The elevation of this escarpment can still be measured by the height of the two knolls of the two great sepulchres which enclose the road from Genappe to Brussels: one, the English tomb, is on the left; the other, the German tomb, is on the right. There is no French tomb. The whole of that plain is a sepulchre for France. Thanks to the thousands upon thousands of cartloads of earth employed in the hillock one hundred and fifty feet in height and half a mile in circumference, the plateau of Mont-Saint-Jean is now accessible by an easy slope. On the day of battle, particularly on the side of La Haie-Sainte, it was abrupt and difficult of approach. The slope there is so steep that the English cannon could not see the farm, situated in the bottom of the valley, which was the centre of the combat. On the 18th of June, 1815, the rains had still farther increased this acclivity, the mud complicated the problem of the ascent, and the men not only slipped back, but stuck fast in the mire. Along the crest of the plateau ran a sort of trench whose presence it was impossible for the distant observer to divine.

What was this trench? Let us explain. Braine-l'Alleud is a Belgian village; Ohain is another. These villages, both of them concealed in curves of the landscape, are connected by a road about a league and a half in length, which traverses the plain along its undulating level, and often enters and buries itself in the hills like a furrow, which makes a ravine of this road in some places. In 1815, as at the present day, this road cut the crest of the plateau of Mont-Saint-Jean between the two highways from Genappe and Nivelles; only, it is now on a level with the plain; it was then a hollow way. Its two slopes have been appropriated for the monumental hillock. This road was, and still is, a trench throughout the greater portion of its course; a hollow trench, sometimes a dozen feet in depth, and whose banks, being too steep, crumbled away here and there, particularly in winter, under driving rains. Accidents happened here. The road was so narrow at the Braine-l'Alleud entrance that a passer-by was crushed by a cart, as is proved by a stone cross which stands near the cemetery, and which gives the name of the dead, Monsieur Bernard Debrye, Merchant of Brussels, and the date of the accident, February, 1637.* It was so deep on the table-land of Mont-Saint-Jean that a peasant, Mathieu Nicaise, was crushed there, in 1783, by a slide from the slope, as is stated on another stone cross, the top of which has disappeared in the process of clearing the ground, but whose overturned pedestal is still visible on the grassy slope to the left of the highway between La Haie-Sainte and the farm of Mont-Saint-Jean.

* This is the inscription:--

    D. O. M.

CY A ETE ECRASE

PAR MALHEUR

SOUS UN CHARIOT,

MONSIEUR BERNARD

DE BRYE MARCHAND

A BRUXELLE LE [Illegible]

FEVRIER 1637.

On the day of battle, this hollow road whose existence was in no way indicated, bordering the crest of Mont-Saint-Jean, a trench at the summit of the escarpment, a rut concealed in the soil, was invisible; that is to say, terrible.

CHAPTER VIII. THE EMPEROR PUTS A QUESTION TO THE GUIDE LACOSTE

So, on the morning of Waterloo, Napoleon was content.

He was right; the plan of battle conceived by him was, as we have seen, really admirable.

The battle once begun, its very various changes,--the resistance of Hougomont; the tenacity of La Haie-Sainte; the killing of Bauduin; the disabling of Foy; the unexpected wall against which Soye's brigade was shattered; Guilleminot's fatal heedlessness when he had neither petard nor powder sacks; the miring of the batteries; the fifteen unescorted pieces overwhelmed in a hollow way by Uxbridge; the small effect of the bombs falling in the English lines, and there embedding themselves in the rain-soaked soil, and only succeeding in producing volcanoes of mud, so that the canister was turned into a splash; the uselessness of Pire's demonstration on Braine-l'Alleud; all that cavalry, fifteen squadrons, almost exterminated; the right wing of the English badly alarmed, the left wing badly cut into; Ney's strange mistake in massing, instead of echelonning the four divisions of the first corps; men delivered over to grape-shot, arranged in ranks twenty-seven deep and with a frontage of two hundred; the frightful holes made in these masses by the cannon-balls; attacking columns disorganized; the side-battery suddenly unmasked on their flank; Bourgeois, Donzelot, and Durutte compromised; Quiot repulsed; Lieutenant Vieux, that Hercules graduated at the Polytechnic School, wounded at the moment when he was beating in with an axe the door of La Haie-Sainte under the downright fire of the English barricade which barred the angle of the road from Genappe to Brussels; Marcognet's division caught between the infantry and the cavalry, shot down at the very

24

muzzle of the guns amid the grain by Best and Pack, put to the sword by Ponsonby; his battery of seven pieces spiked; the Prince of Saxe-Weimar holding and guarding, in spite of the Comte d'Erlon, both Frischemont and Smohain; the flag of the 105th taken, the flag of the 45th captured; that black Prussian hussar stopped by runners of the flying column of three hundred light cavalry on the scout between Wavre and Plancenoit; the alarming things that had been said by prisoners; Grouchy's delay; fifteen hundred men killed in the orchard of Hougomont in less than an hour; eighteen hundred men overthrown in a still shorter time about La Haie-Sainte,--all these stormy incidents passing like the clouds of battle before Napoleon, had hardly troubled his gaze and had not overshadowed that face of imperial certainty. Napoleon was accustomed to gaze steadily at war; he never added up the heart-rending details, cipher by cipher; ciphers mattered little to him, provided that they furnished the total, victory; he was not alarmed if the beginnings did go astray, since he thought himself the master and the possessor at the end; he knew how to wait, supposing himself to be out of the question, and he treated destiny as his equal: he seemed to say to fate, Thou wilt not dare.

Composed half of light and half of shadow, Napoleon thought himself protected in good and tolerated in evil. He had, or thought that he had, a connivance, one might almost say a complicity, of events in his favor, which was equivalent to the invulnerability of antiquity.

Nevertheless, when one has Beresina, Leipzig, and Fontainebleau behind one, it seems as though one might distrust Waterloo. A mysterious frown becomes perceptible in the depths of the heavens.

At the moment when Wellington retreated, Napoleon shuddered. He suddenly beheld the table-land of Mont-Saint-Jean cleared, and the van of the English army disappear. It was rallying, but hiding itself. The Emperor half rose in his stirrups. The lightning of victory flashed from his eyes.

Wellington, driven into a corner at the forest of Soignes and destroyed--that was the definitive conquest of England by France; it was Crecy, Poitiers, Malplaquet, and Ramillies avenged. The man of Marengo was wiping out Agincourt.

So the Emperor, meditating on this terrible turn of fortune, swept his glass for the last time over all the points of the field of battle. His guard, standing behind him with grounded arms, watched him from below with a sort of religion. He pondered; he examined the slopes, noted the declivities, scrutinized the clumps of trees, the square of rye, the path; he seemed to be counting each bush. He gazed with some intentness at the English barricades of the two highways,--two large abatis of trees, that on the road to Genappe above La Haie-Sainte, armed with two cannon, the only ones out of all the English artillery which commanded the extremity of the field of battle, and that on the road to Nivelles where gleamed the Dutch bayonets of Chasse's brigade. Near this barricade he observed the old chapel of Saint Nicholas, painted white, which stands at the angle of the cross-road near Braine l'Alleud; he bent down and spoke in a low voice to the guide Lacoste. The guide made a negative sign with his head, which was probably perfidious.

The Emperor straightened himself up and fell to thinking.

Wellington had drawn back.

All that remained to do was to complete this retreat by crushing him.

Napoleon turning round abruptly, despatched an express at full speed to Paris to announce that the battle was won.

Napoleon was one of those geniuses from whom thunder darts.

He had just found his clap of thunder.

He gave orders to Milhaud's cuirassiers to carry the table-land of Mont-Saint-Jean.

CHAPTER IX. THE UNEXPECTED

There were three thousand five hundred of them. They formed a front a quarter of a league in extent. They were giant men, on colossal horses. There were six and twenty squadrons of them; and they had behind them to support them Lefebvre-Desnouettes's division,--the one hundred and six picked gendarmes, the light cavalry of the Guard, eleven hundred and ninety-seven men, and the lancers of the guard of eight hundred and eighty lances. They wore casques without horse-tails, and cuirasses of beaten iron, with horse-pistols in their holsters, and long sabre-swords. That morning the whole army had admired them, when, at nine o'clock, with braying of trumpets and all the music playing "Let us watch o'er the Safety of the Empire," they had come in a solid column, with one of their batteries on their flank, another in their centre, and deployed in two ranks between the roads to Genappe and Frischemont, and taken up their position for battle in that powerful second line, so cleverly arranged by Napoleon, which, having on its extreme left Kellermann's cuirassiers and on its extreme right Milhaud's cuirassiers, had, so to speak, two wings of iron.

Aide-de-camp Bernard carried them the Emperor's orders. Ney drew his sword and placed himself at their head. The enormous squadrons were set in motion.

Then a formidable spectacle was seen.

All their cavalry, with upraised swords, standards and trumpets flung to the breeze, formed in columns by divisions, descended, by a simultaneous movement and like one man, with the precision of a brazen battering-ram which is effecting a breach, the hill of La Belle Alliance, plunged into the terrible depths in which so many men had already fallen, disappeared there in the smoke, then emerging from that shadow, reappeared on the other side of the valley, still compact and in close ranks, mounting at a full trot, through a storm of grape-shot which burst upon them, the terrible muddy slope of the table-land of Mont-Saint-Jean. They ascended, grave, threatening, imperturbable; in the intervals between the musketry and the artillery, their colossal trampling was audible. Being two divisions, there were two columns of them; Wathier's division held the right, Delort's division was on the left. It seemed as though two immense adders of steel were to be seen crawling towards the crest of the table-land. It traversed the battle like a prodigy.

Nothing like it had been seen since the taking of the great redoubt of the Muskowa by the heavy cavalry; Murat was lacking here, but Ney was again present. It seemed as though that mass had become a monster and had but one soul. Each column undulated and swelled like the ring of a polyp. They could be seen through a vast cloud of smoke which was rent here and there. A confusion of helmets, of cries, of sabres, a stormy heaving of the cruppers of horses amid the cannons and the flourish of trumpets, a terrible and disciplined tumult; over all, the cuirasses like the scales on the hydra.

These narrations seemed to belong to another age. Something parallel to this vision appeared, no doubt, in the ancient Orphic epics, which told of the centaurs, the old hippanthropes, those Titans with human heads and equestrian chests who scaled Olympus at a gallop, horrible, invulnerable, sublime--gods and beasts.

Odd numerical coincidence,--twenty-six battalions rode to meet twenty-six battalions. Behind the crest of the plateau, in the shadow of the masked battery, the English infantry, formed into thirteen squares, two battalions to the square, in two lines, with seven in the first line, six in the second, the stocks of their guns to their shoulders, taking aim at that which was on the point of appearing, waited, calm, mute, motionless. They did not see the cuirassiers, and the cuirassiers did not see them. They listened to the rise of this flood of men. They heard the swelling noise of three thousand horse, the alternate and symmetrical tramp of their hoofs at full trot, the jingling of the cuirasses, the clang of the sabres and a sort of grand and savage breathing. There ensued a most terrible silence; then, all at once, a long file of uplifted arms, brandishing sabres, appeared above the crest, and casques, trumpets, and standards, and three thousand heads with gray mustaches, shouting, "Vive l'Empereur!" All this cavalry debouched on the plateau, and it was like the appearance of an earthquake.

All at once, a tragic incident; on the English left, on our right, the head of the column of cuirassiers reared up with a frightful clamor. On arriving at the culminating point of the crest, ungovernable, utterly given over to fury and their course of extermination of the squares and cannon, the cuirassiers had just caught sight of a trench,-- a trench between them and the English. It was the hollow road of Ohain.

It was a terrible moment. The ravine was there, unexpected, yawning, directly under the horses' feet, two fathoms deep between its double slopes; the second file pushed the first into it, and the third pushed on the second; the horses reared and fell backward, landed on their haunches, slid down, all four feet in the air, crushing and overwhelming the riders; and there being no means of retreat,-- the whole column being no longer anything more than a projectile,-- the force which had been acquired to crush the English crushed the French; the inexorable ravine could only yield when filled; horses and riders rolled there pell-mell, grinding each other, forming but one mass of flesh in this gulf: when this trench was full of living men, the rest marched over them and passed on. Almost a third of Dubois's brigade fell into that abyss.

This began the loss of the battle.

A local tradition, which evidently exaggerates matters, says that two thousand horses and fifteen hundred men were buried in the hollow road of Ohain. This figure probably comprises all the other corpses which were flung into this ravine the day after the combat.

Let us note in passing that it was Dubois's sorely tried brigade which, an hour previously, making a charge to one side, had captured the flag of the Lunenburg battalion.

Napoleon, before giving the order for this charge of Milhaud's cuirassiers, had scrutinized the ground, but had not been able to see that hollow road, which did not even form a wrinkle on the surface of the plateau. Warned, nevertheless, and put on the alert by the little white chapel which marks its angle of junction with the Nivelles highway, he had probably put a question as to the possibility of an obstacle, to the guide Lacoste. The guide had answered No. We might almost affirm that Napoleon's catastrophe originated in that sign of a peasant's head.

Other fatalities were destined to arise.

Was it possible that Napoleon should have won that battle? We answer No. Why? Because of Wellington? Because of Blucher? No. Because of God.

Bonaparte victor at Waterloo; that does not come within the law of the nineteenth century. Another series of facts was in preparation, in which there was no longer any room for Napoleon. The ill will of events had declared itself long before.

It was time that this vast man should fall.

The excessive weight of this man in human destiny disturbed the balance. This individual alone counted for more than a universal group. These plethoras of all human vitality concentrated in a single head; the world mounting to the brain of one man,--this would be mortal to civilization were it to last. The moment had arrived for the incorruptible and supreme equity to alter its plan. Probably the principles and the elements, on which the regular gravitations of the moral, as of the material, world depend, had complained. Smoking blood, over-filled cemeteries, mothers in tears,-- these are formidable pleaders. When the earth is suffering from too heavy a burden, there are mysterious groanings of the shades, to which the abyss lends an ear.

Napoleon had been denounced in the infinite and his fall had been decided on.

He embarrassed God.

Waterloo is not a battle; it is a change of front on the part of the Universe.

CHAPTER X. THE PLATEAU OF MONT-SAINT-JEAN

The battery was unmasked at the same moment with the ravine.

Sixty cannons and the thirteen squares darted lightning point-blank on the cuirassiers. The intrepid General Delort made the military salute to the English battery.

The whole of the flying artillery of the English had re-entered the squares at a gallop. The cuirassiers had not had even the time for a halt. The disaster of the hollow road had decimated, but not discouraged them. They belonged to that class of men who, when diminished in number, increase in courage.

Wathier's column alone had suffered in the disaster; Delort's column, which Ney had deflected to the left, as though he had a presentiment of an ambush, had arrived whole.

29

The cuirassiers hurled themselves on the English squares.

At full speed, with bridles loose, swords in their teeth pistols in fist,--such was the attack.

There are moments in battles in which the soul hardens the man until the soldier is changed into a statue, and when all this flesh turns into granite. The English battalions, desperately assaulted, did not stir.

Then it was terrible.

All the faces of the English squares were attacked at once. A frenzied whirl enveloped them. That cold infantry remained impassive. The first rank knelt and received the cuirassiers on their bayonets, the second ranks shot them down; behind the second rank the cannoneers charged their guns, the front of the square parted, permitted the passage of an eruption of grape-shot, and closed again. The cuirassiers replied by crushing them. Their great horses reared, strode across the ranks, leaped over the bayonets and fell, gigantic, in the midst of these four living wells. The cannon-balls ploughed furrows in these cuirassiers; the cuirassiers made breaches in the squares. Files of men disappeared, ground to dust under the horses. The bayonets plunged into the bellies of these centaurs; hence a hideousness of wounds which has probably never been seen anywhere else. The squares, wasted by this mad cavalry, closed up their ranks without flinching. Inexhaustible in the matter of grape-shot, they created explosions in their assailants' midst. The form of this combat was monstrous. These squares were no longer battalions, they were craters; those cuirassiers were no longer cavalry, they were a tempest. Each square was a volcano attacked by a cloud; lava contended with lightning.

The square on the extreme right, the most exposed of all, being in the air, was almost annihilated at the very first shock. It was formed of the 75th regiment of Highlanders. The bagpipe-player in the centre dropped his melancholy eyes, filled with the reflections of the forests and the lakes, in profound inattention, while men were being exterminated around him, and seated on a drum, with his pibroch under his arm, played the Highland airs. These Scotchmen died thinking of Ben Lothian, as did the Greeks recalling Argos. The sword of a cuirassier, which hewed down the bagpipes and the arm which bore it, put an end to the song by killing the singer.

The cuirassiers, relatively few in number, and still further diminished by the catastrophe of the ravine, had almost the whole English army against them, but they multiplied themselves so that each man of them was equal to ten. Nevertheless, some Hanoverian battalions yielded. Wellington perceived it, and thought of his cavalry. Had Napoleon at that same moment thought of his infantry, he would have won the battle. This forgetfulness was his great and fatal mistake.

All at once, the cuirassiers, who had been the assailants, found themselves assailed. The English cavalry was at their back. Before them two squares, behind them Somerset; Somerset meant fourteen hundred dragoons of the guard. On the right, Somerset had Dornberg with the German light-horse, and on his left, Trip with the Belgian carabineers; the cuirassiers attacked on the flank and in front, before and in the rear, by infantry and cavalry, had to face all sides. What mattered it to them? They were a whirlwind. Their valor was something indescribable.

In addition to this, they had behind them the battery, which was still thundering. It was necessary that it should be so, or they could never have been wounded in the back. One of their cuirasses, pierced on the shoulder by a ball from a biscayan,[3] is in the collection of the Waterloo Museum.

For such Frenchmen nothing less than such Englishmen was needed. It was no longer a hand-to-hand conflict; it was a shadow, a fury, a dizzy transport of souls and courage, a hurricane of lightning swords. In an instant the fourteen hundred dragoon guards numbered only eight hundred. Fuller, their lieutenant-colonel, fell dead. Ney rushed up with the lancers and Lefebvre-Desnouettes's light-horse. The plateau of Mont-Saint-Jean was captured, recaptured, captured again. The cuirassiers quitted the cavalry to return to the infantry; or, to put it more exactly, the whole of that formidable rout collared each other without releasing the other. The squares still held firm.

There were a dozen assaults. Ney had four horses killed under him. Half the cuirassiers remained on the plateau. This conflict lasted two hours.

The English army was profoundly shaken. There is no doubt that, had they not been enfeebled in their first shock by the disaster of the hollow road the cuirassiers would have overwhelmed the centre and decided the victory. This extraordinary cavalry petrified Clinton, who had seen Talavera and Badajoz. Wellington, three-quarters vanquished, admired heroically. He said in an undertone, "Sublime!"

The cuirassiers annihilated seven squares out of thirteen, took or spiked sixty pieces of ordnance, and captured from the English regiments six flags, which three cuirassiers and three chasseurs of the Guard bore to the Emperor, in front of the farm of La Belle Alliance.

---

3   A heavy rifled gun.

Wellington's situation had grown worse. This strange battle was like a duel between two raging, wounded men, each of whom, still fighting and still resisting, is expending all his blood.

Which of the two will be the first to fall?

The conflict on the plateau continued.

What had become of the cuirassiers? No one could have told. One thing is certain, that on the day after the battle, a cuirassier and his horse were found dead among the woodwork of the scales for vehicles at Mont-Saint-Jean, at the very point where the four roads from Nivelles, Genappe, La Hulpe, and Brussels meet and intersect each other. This horseman had pierced the English lines. One of the men who picked up the body still lives at Mont-Saint-Jean. His name is Dehaze. He was eighteen years old at that time.

Wellington felt that he was yielding. The crisis was at hand.

The cuirassiers had not succeeded, since the centre was not broken through. As every one was in possession of the plateau, no one held it, and in fact it remained, to a great extent, with the English. Wellington held the village and the culminating plain; Ney had only the crest and the slope. They seemed rooted in that fatal soil on both sides.

But the weakening of the English seemed irremediable. The bleeding of that army was horrible. Kempt, on the left wing, demanded reinforcements. "There are none," replied Wellington; "he must let himself be killed!" Almost at that same moment, a singular coincidence which paints the exhaustion of the two armies, Ney demanded infantry from Napoleon, and Napoleon exclaimed, "Infantry! Where does he expect me to get it? Does he think I can make it?"

Nevertheless, the English army was in the worse case of the two. The furious onsets of those great squadrons with cuirasses of iron and breasts of steel had ground the infantry to nothing. A few men clustered round a flag marked the post of a regiment; such and such a battalion was commanded only by a captain or a lieutenant; Alten's division, already so roughly handled at La Haie-Sainte, was almost destroyed; the intrepid Belgians of Van Kluze's brigade strewed the rye-fields all along the Nivelles road; hardly anything was left of those Dutch grenadiers, who, intermingled with Spaniards in our ranks in 1811, fought against Wellington; and who, in 1815, rallied to the English standard, fought against Napoleon. The loss in officers was considerable. Lord Uxbridge, who had his leg buried on the following day, had his knee shattered. If, on the French side, in that tussle of the cuirassiers, Delort, l'Heritier, Colbert, Dnop, Travers,

32

and Blancard were disabled, on the side of the English there was Alten wounded, Barne wounded, Delancey killed, Van Meeren killed, Ompteda killed, the whole of Wellington's staff decimated, and England had the worse of it in that bloody scale. The second regiment of foot-guards had lost five lieutenant-colonels, four captains, and three ensigns; the first battalion of the 30th infantry had lost 24 officers and 1,200 soldiers; the 79th Highlanders had lost 24 officers wounded, 18 officers killed, 450 soldiers killed. The Hanoverian hussars of Cumberland, a whole regiment, with Colonel Hacke at its head, who was destined to be tried later on and cashiered, had turned bridle in the presence of the fray, and had fled to the forest of Soignes, sowing defeat all the way to Brussels. The transports, ammunition-wagons, the baggage-wagons, the wagons filled with wounded, on perceiving that the French were gaining ground and approaching the forest, rushed headlong thither. The Dutch, mowed down by the French cavalry, cried, "Alarm!" From Vert-Coucou to Groentendael, for a distance of nearly two leagues in the direction of Brussels, according to the testimony of eye-witnesses who are still alive, the roads were encumbered with fugitives. This panic was such that it attacked the Prince de Conde at Mechlin, and Louis XVIII. at Ghent. With the exception of the feeble reserve echelonned behind the ambulance established at the farm of Mont-Saint-Jean, and of Vivian's and Vandeleur's brigades, which flanked the left wing, Wellington had no cavalry left. A number of batteries lay unhorsed. These facts are attested by Siborne; and Pringle, exaggerating the disaster, goes so far as to say that the Anglo-Dutch army was reduced to thirty-four thousand men. The Iron Duke remained calm, but his lips blanched. Vincent, the Austrian commissioner, Alava, the Spanish commissioner, who were present at the battle in the English staff, thought the Duke lost. At five o'clock Wellington drew out his watch, and he was heard to murmur these sinister words, "Blucher, or night!"

It was at about that moment that a distant line of bayonets gleamed on the heights in the direction of Frischemont.

Here comes the change of face in this giant drama.

CHAPTER XI. A BAD GUIDE TO NAPOLEON; A GOOD GUIDE TO BULOW

The painful surprise of Napoleon is well known. Grouchy hoped for, Blucher arriving. Death instead of life.

Fate has these turns; the throne of the world was expected; it was Saint Helena that was seen.

If the little shepherd who served as guide to Bulow, Blucher's lieutenant, had advised him to debouch from the forest above Frischemont, instead of below Plancenoit, the form of the nineteenth century might, perhaps, have been different. Napoleon would have won the battle of Waterloo. By any other route than that below Plancenoit, the Prussian army would have come out upon a ravine impassable for artillery, and Bulow would not have arrived.

Now the Prussian general, Muffling, declares that one hour's delay, and Blucher would not have found Wellington on his feet. "The battle was lost."

It was time that Bulow should arrive, as will be seen. He had, moreover, been very much delayed. He had bivouacked at Dion-le-Mont, and had set out at daybreak; but the roads were impassable, and his divisions stuck fast in the mire. The ruts were up to the hubs of the cannons. Moreover, he had been obliged to pass the Dyle on the narrow bridge of Wavre; the street leading to the bridge had been fired by the French, so the caissons and ammunition-wagons could not pass between two rows of burning houses, and had been obliged to wait until the conflagration was extinguished. It was mid-day before Bulow's vanguard had been able to reach Chapelle-Saint-Lambert.

Had the action been begun two hours earlier, it would have been over at four o'clock, and Blucher would have fallen on the battle won by Napoleon. Such are these immense risks proportioned to an infinite which we cannot comprehend.

The Emperor had been the first, as early as mid-day, to descry with his field-glass, on the extreme horizon, something which had attracted his attention. He had said, "I see yonder a cloud, which seems to me to be troops." Then he asked the Duc de Dalmatie, "Soult, what do you see in the direction of Chapelle-Saint-Lambert?" The marshal, levelling his glass, answered, "Four or five thousand men, Sire; evidently Grouchy." But it remained motionless in the mist. All the glasses of the staff had studied "the cloud" pointed out by the Emperor. Some said: "It is trees." The truth is, that the cloud did not move. The Emperor detached Domon's division of light cavalry to reconnoitre in that quarter.

Bulow had not moved, in fact. His vanguard was very feeble, and could accomplish nothing. He was obliged to wait for the body of the army corps, and he had received orders to concentrate his forces before entering into line; but at five o'clock, perceiving Wellington's peril, Blucher ordered Bulow to attack, and uttered these remarkable words: "We must give air to the English army."

A little later, the divisions of Losthin, Hiller, Hacke, and Ryssel deployed before Lobau's corps, the cavalry of Prince William of Prussia debouched from the forest of Paris, Plancenoit was in flames, and the Prussian cannon-balls began to rain even upon the ranks of the guard in reserve behind Napoleon.

CHAPTER XII. THE GUARD

Every one knows the rest,--the irruption of a third army; the battle broken to pieces; eighty-six months of fire thundering simultaneously; Pirch the first coming up with Bulow; Zieten's cavalry led by Blucher in person, the French driven back; Marcognet swept from the plateau of Ohain; Durutte dislodged from Papelotte; Donzelot and Quiot retreating; Lobau caught on the flank; a fresh battle precipitating itself on our dismantled regiments at nightfall; the whole English line resuming the offensive and thrust forward; the gigantic breach made in the French army; the English grape-shot and the Prussian grape-shot aiding each other; the extermination; disaster in front; disaster on the flank; the Guard entering the line in the midst of this terrible crumbling of all things.

Conscious that they were about to die, they shouted, "Vive l'Empereur!" History records nothing more touching than that agony bursting forth in acclamations.

The sky had been overcast all day long. All of a sudden, at that very moment,--it was eight o'clock in the evening--the clouds on the horizon parted, and allowed the grand and sinister glow of the setting sun to pass through, athwart the elms on the Nivelles road. They had seen it rise at Austerlitz.

Each battalion of the Guard was commanded by a general for this final catastrophe. Friant, Michel, Roguet, Harlet, Mallet, Poret de Morvan, were there. When the tall caps of the grenadiers of the Guard, with their large plaques bearing the eagle appeared, symmetrical, in line, tranquil, in the midst of that combat, the enemy felt a respect for France; they thought they beheld twenty victories entering the field of battle, with wings outspread, and those who were the conquerors, believing themselves to be vanquished, retreated; but Wellington shouted, "Up, Guards, and aim straight!" The red regiment of English guards, lying flat behind the hedges, sprang up, a cloud of grape-shot riddled the tricolored flag and whistled round our eagles; all hurled themselves forwards, and the final carnage began. In the darkness, the Imperial Guard felt the army losing ground around it, and in the vast shock of the rout it heard the desperate flight which had taken the place of the "Vive l'Empereur!" and, with flight behind it, it continued to advance, more crushed, losing more men at every step that it took. There were none who hesitated, no timid men in its ranks. The soldier in that troop was as much of a hero as the general. Not a man was missing in that suicide.

Ney, bewildered, great with all the grandeur of accepted death, offered himself to all blows in that tempest. He had his fifth horse killed under him there. Perspiring, his eyes aflame, foaming at the mouth, with uniform unbuttoned, one of his epaulets half cut off by a sword-stroke from a horseguard, his plaque with the great eagle dented by a bullet; bleeding, bemired, magnificent, a broken sword in his hand, he said, "Come and see how a Marshal of France dies on the field of battle!" But in vain; he did not die. He was haggard and angry. At Drouet d'Erlon he hurled this question, "Are you not going to get yourself killed?" In the midst of all that artillery engaged in crushing a handful of men, he shouted: "So there is nothing for me! Oh! I should like to have all these English bullets enter my bowels!" Unhappy man, thou wert reserved for French bullets!

CHAPTER XIII. THE CATASTROPHE

The rout behind the Guard was melancholy.

The army yielded suddenly on all sides at once,--Hougomont, La Haie-Sainte, Papelotte, Plancenoit. The cry "Treachery!" was followed by a cry of "Save yourselves who can!" An army which is disbanding is like a thaw. All yields, splits, cracks, floats, rolls, falls, jostles, hastens, is precipitated. The disintegration is unprecedented. Ney borrows a horse, leaps upon it, and without hat, cravat, or sword, places himself across the Brussels road, stopping both English and French. He strives to detain the army, he recalls it to its duty, he insults it, he clings to the rout. He is overwhelmed. The soldiers fly from him, shouting, "Long live Marshal Ney!" Two of Durutte's regiments go and come in affright as though tossed back and forth between the swords of the Uhlans and the fusillade of the brigades of Kempt, Best, Pack, and Rylandt; the worst of hand-to-hand conflicts is the defeat; friends kill each other in order to escape; squadrons and battalions break and disperse against each other, like the tremendous foam of battle. Lobau at one extremity, and Reille at the other, are drawn into the tide. In vain does Napoleon erect walls from what is left to him of his Guard; in vain does he expend in a last effort his last serviceable squadrons. Quiot retreats before Vivian, Kellermann before Vandeleur, Lobau before Bulow, Morand before Pirch, Domon and Subervic before Prince William of Prussia; Guyot, who led the Emperor's squadrons to the charge, falls beneath the feet of the English dragoons. Napoleon gallops past the line of fugitives, harangues, urges, threatens, entreats them. All the mouths which in the morning had shouted, "Long live the Emperor!" remain gaping; they hardly recognize him. The Prussian cavalry, newly arrived, dashes forwards, flies, hews, slashes, kills, exterminates. Horses lash out, the cannons flee; the soldiers of the artillery-train unharness the caissons and use the horses to make their escape; transports overturned, with all four wheels in the air, clog the road and occasion massacres. Men are crushed, trampled down, others walk over the dead and the living. Arms are lost. A dizzy multitude fills the roads, the paths, the bridges, the plains, the hills, the valleys, the woods, encumbered by this invasion of forty thousand men. Shouts despair, knapsacks and guns flung among the rye, passages forced at the point of the sword, no more comrades, no more officers, no more generals, an inexpressible terror. Zieten putting France to the sword at its leisure. Lions converted into goats. Such was the flight.

At Genappe, an effort was made to wheel about, to present a battle front, to draw up in line. Lobau rallied three hundred men. The entrance to the village was barricaded, but at the first volley of Prussian canister, all took to flight again, and Lobau was taken. That volley of grape-shot can be seen to-day imprinted on the ancient gable of a brick building on the right of the road at a few minutes' distance before you enter Genappe. The Prussians threw themselves into Genappe, furious, no doubt, that they were not more entirely the conquerors. The pursuit was stupendous. Blucher ordered extermination. Roguet had set the lugubrious example of threatening with death any French grenadier who should bring him a Prussian prisoner. Blucher outdid Roguet. Duhesme, the general of the Young Guard, hemmed in at the doorway of an inn at Genappe, surrendered his sword to a huzzar of death, who took the sword and slew the prisoner. The victory was completed by the assassination of the vanquished. Let us inflict punishment, since we are history: old Blucher disgraced himself. This ferocity put the finishing touch to the disaster. The desperate route traversed Genappe, traversed Quatre-Bras, traversed Gosselies, traversed Frasnes, traversed Charleroi, traversed Thuin, and only halted at the frontier. Alas! and who, then, was fleeing in that manner? The Grand Army.

This vertigo, this terror, this downfall into ruin of the loftiest bravery which ever astounded history,--is that causeless? No. The shadow of an enormous right is projected athwart Waterloo. It is the day of destiny. The force which is mightier than man produced that day. Hence the terrified wrinkle of those brows; hence all those great souls surrendering their swords. Those who had conquered Europe have fallen prone on the earth, with nothing left to say nor to do, feeling the present shadow of a terrible presence. Hoc erat in fatis. That day the perspective of the human race underwent a change. Waterloo is the hinge of the nineteenth century. The disappearance of the great man was necessary to the advent of the great century. Some one, a person to whom one replies not, took the responsibility on himself. The panic of heroes can be explained. In the battle of Waterloo there is something more than a cloud, there is something of the meteor. God has passed by.

At nightfall, in a meadow near Genappe, Bernard and Bertrand seized by the skirt of his coat and detained a man, haggard, pensive, sinister, gloomy, who, dragged to that point by the current of the rout, had just dismounted, had passed the bridle of his horse over his arm, and with wild eye was returning alone to Waterloo. It was Napoleon, the immense somnambulist of this dream which had crumbled, essaying once more to advance.

CHAPTER XIV. THE LAST SQUARE

Several squares of the Guard, motionless amid this stream of the defeat, as rocks in running water, held their own until night. Night came, death also; they awaited that double shadow, and, invincible, allowed themselves to be enveloped therein. Each regiment, isolated from the rest, and having no bond with the army, now shattered in every part, died alone. They had taken up position for this final action, some on the heights of Rossomme, others on the plain of Mont-Saint-Jean. There, abandoned, vanquished, terrible, those gloomy squares endured their death-throes in formidable fashion. Ulm, Wagram, Jena, Friedland, died with them.

At twilight, towards nine o'clock in the evening, one of them was left at the foot of the plateau of Mont-Saint-Jean. In that fatal valley, at the foot of that declivity which the cuirassiers had ascended, now inundated by the masses of the English, under the converging fires of the victorious hostile cavalry, under a frightful density of projectiles, this square fought on. It was commanded by an obscure officer named Cambronne. At each discharge, the square diminished and replied. It replied to the grape-shot with a fusillade, continually contracting its four walls. The fugitives pausing breathless for a moment in the distance, listened in the darkness to that gloomy and ever-decreasing thunder.

When this legion had been reduced to a handful, when nothing was left of their flag but a rag, when their guns, the bullets all gone, were no longer anything but clubs, when the heap of corpses was larger than the group of survivors, there reigned among the conquerors, around those men dying so sublimely, a sort of sacred terror, and the English artillery, taking breath, became silent. This furnished a sort of respite. These combatants had around them something in the nature of a swarm of spectres, silhouettes of men on horseback, the black profiles of cannon, the white sky viewed through wheels and gun-carriages, the colossal death's-head, which the heroes saw constantly through the smoke, in the depths of the battle, advanced upon them and gazed at them. Through the shades of twilight they could hear the pieces being loaded; the matches all lighted, like the eyes of tigers at night, formed a circle round their heads; all the lintstocks of the English batteries approached the cannons, and then, with emotion, holding the supreme moment suspended above these men, an English general, Colville according to some, Maitland according to others, shouted to them, "Surrender, brave Frenchmen!" Cambronne replied, "-----."

{EDITOR'S COMMENTARY: Another edition of this book has the word "Merde!" in lieu of the ----- above.}

CHAPTER XV. CAMBRONNE

If any French reader object to having his susceptibilities offended, one would have to refrain from repeating in his presence what is perhaps the finest reply that a Frenchman ever made. This would enjoin us from consigning something sublime to History.

At our own risk and peril, let us violate this injunction.

Now, then, among those giants there was one Titan,--Cambronne.

To make that reply and then perish, what could be grander? For being willing to die is the same as to die; and it was not this man's fault if he survived after he was shot.

The winner of the battle of Waterloo was not Napoleon, who was put to flight; nor Wellington, giving way at four o'clock, in despair at five; nor Blucher, who took no part in the engagement. The winner of Waterloo was Cambronne.

To thunder forth such a reply at the lightning-flash that kills you is to conquer!

Thus to answer the Catastrophe, thus to speak to Fate, to give this pedestal to the future lion, to hurl such a challenge to the midnight rainstorm, to the treacherous wall of Hougomont, to the sunken road of Ohain, to Grouchy's delay, to Blucher's arrival, to be Irony itself in the tomb, to act so as to stand upright though fallen, to drown in two syllables the European coalition, to offer kings privies which the Caesars once knew, to make the lowest of words the most lofty by entwining with it the glory of France, insolently to end Waterloo with Mardigras, to finish Leonidas with Rabellais, to set the crown on this victory by a word impossible to speak, to lose the field and preserve history, to have the laugh on your side after such a carnage,--this is immense!

It was an insult such as a thunder-cloud might hurl! It reaches the grandeur of AEschylus!

Cambronne's reply produces the effect of a violent break. 'Tis like the breaking of a heart under a weight of scorn. 'Tis the overflow of agony bursting forth. Who conquered? Wellington? No! Had it not been for Blucher, he was lost. Was it Blucher? No! If Wellington had not begun, Blucher could not have finished. This Cambronne, this man spending his last hour, this unknown soldier, this infinitesimal of war, realizes that here is a falsehood, a falsehood in a catastrophe, and so doubly agonizing; and at the moment when his rage is bursting forth because of it, he is offered this mockery,--life! How could he restrain himself? Yonder are all the kings of Europe, the general's flushed with victory, the Jupiter's darting thunderbolts; they have a hundred thousand victorious soldiers, and back of the hundred thousand a million; their cannon stand with yawning mouths, the match is lighted; they grind down under their heels the Imperial guards, and the grand army; they have just crushed Napoleon, and only Cambronne remains,-- only this earthworm is left to protest. He will protest. Then he seeks for the appropriate word as one seeks for a sword. His mouth froths, and the froth is the word. In face of this mean and mighty victory, in face of this victory which counts none victorious, this desperate soldier stands erect. He grants its overwhelming immensity, but he establishes its triviality; and he does more than spit upon it. Borne down by numbers, by superior force, by brute matter, he finds in his soul an expression: "Excrement!" We repeat it,-- to use that word, to do thus, to invent such an expression, is to be the conqueror!

The spirit of mighty days at that portentous moment made its descent on that unknown man. Cambronne invents the word for Waterloo as Rouget invents the "Marseillaise," under the visitation of a breath from on high. An emanation from the divine whirlwind leaps forth and comes sweeping over these men, and they shake, and one of them sings the song supreme, and the other utters the frightful cry.

This challenge of titanic scorn Cambronne hurls not only at Europe in the name of the Empire,--that would be a trifle: he hurls it at the past in the name of the Revolution. It is heard, and Cambronne is recognized as possessed by the ancient spirit of the Titans. Danton seems to be speaking! Kleber seems to be bellowing!

At that word from Cambronne, the English voice responded, "Fire!" The batteries flamed, the hill trembled, from all those brazen mouths belched a last terrible gush of grape-shot; a vast volume of smoke, vaguely white in the light of the rising moon, rolled out, and when the smoke dispersed, there was no longer anything there. That formidable remnant had been annihilated; the Guard was dead. The four walls of the living redoubt lay prone, and hardly was there discernible, here and there, even a quiver in the bodies; it was thus that the French legions, greater than the Roman legions, expired on Mont-Saint-Jean, on the soil watered with rain and blood, amid the gloomy grain, on the spot where nowadays Joseph, who drives the post-wagon from Nivelles, passes whistling, and cheerfully whipping up his horse at four o'clock in the morning.

CHAPTER XVI. QUOT LIBRAS IN DUCE?

The battle of Waterloo is an enigma. It is as obscure to those who won it as to those who lost it. For Napoleon it was a panic;[4] Blucher sees nothing in it but fire; Wellington understands nothing in regard to it. Look at the reports. The bulletins are confused, the commentaries involved. Some stammer, others lisp. Jomini divides the battle of Waterloo into four moments; Muffling cuts it up into three changes; Charras alone, though we hold another judgment than his on some points, seized with his haughty glance the characteristic outlines of that catastrophe of human genius in conflict with divine chance. All the other historians suffer from being somewhat dazzled, and in this dazzled state they fumble about. It was a day of lightning brilliancy; in fact, a crumbling of the military monarchy which, to the vast stupefaction of kings, drew all the kingdoms after it--the fall of force, the defeat of war.

In this event, stamped with superhuman necessity, the part played by men amounts to nothing.

If we take Waterloo from Wellington and Blucher, do we thereby deprive England and Germany of anything? No. Neither that illustrious England nor that august Germany enter into the problem of Waterloo. Thank Heaven, nations are great, independently of the lugubrious feats of the sword. Neither England, nor Germany, nor France is contained in a scabbard. At this epoch when Waterloo is only a clashing of swords, above Blucher, Germany has Schiller; above Wellington, England has Byron. A vast dawn of ideas is the peculiarity of our century, and in that aurora England and Germany have a magnificent radiance. They are majestic because they think. The elevation of level which they contribute to civilization is intrinsic with them; it proceeds from themselves and not from an accident. The aggrandizement which they have brought to the nineteenth century has not Waterloo as its source. It is only barbarous peoples who undergo rapid growth after a victory. That is the temporary vanity of torrents swelled by a storm. Civilized people, especially in our day, are neither elevated nor abased by the good or bad fortune of a captain.

---

4   "A battle terminated, a day finished, false measures repaired, greater successes assured for the morrow,--all was lost by a moment of panic, terror."--Napoleon, Dictees de Sainte Helene.

Their specific gravity in the human species results from something more than a combat. Their honor, thank God! their dignity, their intelligence, their genius, are not numbers which those gamblers, heroes and conquerors, can put in the lottery of battles. Often a battle is lost and progress is conquered. There is less glory and more liberty. The drum holds its peace; reason takes the word. It is a game in which he who loses wins. Let us, therefore, speak of Waterloo coldly from both sides. Let us render to chance that which is due to chance, and to God that which is due to God. What is Waterloo? A victory? No. The winning number in the lottery.

The quine[5] won by Europe, paid by France.

It was not worth while to place a lion there.

Waterloo, moreover, is the strangest encounter in history. Napoleon and Wellington. They are not enemies; they are opposites. Never did God, who is fond of antitheses, make a more striking contrast, a more extraordinary comparison. On one side, precision, foresight, geometry, prudence, an assured retreat, reserves spared, with an obstinate coolness, an imperturbable method, strategy, which takes advantage of the ground, tactics, which preserve the equilibrium of battalions, carnage, executed according to rule, war regulated, watch in hand, nothing voluntarily left to chance, the ancient classic courage, absolute regularity; on the other, intuition, divination, military oddity, superhuman instinct, a flaming glance, an indescribable something which gazes like an eagle, and which strikes like the lightning, a prodigious art in disdainful impetuosity, all the mysteries of a profound soul, associated with destiny; the stream, the plain, the forest, the hill, summoned, and in a manner, forced to obey, the despot going even so far as to tyrannize over the field of battle; faith in a star mingled with strategic science, elevating but perturbing it. Wellington was the Bareme of war; Napoleon was its Michael Angelo; and on this occasion, genius was vanquished by calculation. On both sides some one was awaited. It was the exact calculator who succeeded. Napoleon was waiting for Grouchy; he did not come. Wellington expected Blucher; he came.

Wellington is classic war taking its revenge. Bonaparte, at his dawning, had encountered him in Italy, and beaten him superbly. The old owl had fled before the young vulture. The old tactics had been not only struck as by lightning, but disgraced. Who was that Corsican of six and twenty? What signified that splendid ignoramus, who, with everything against him, nothing in his favor, without provisions, without ammunition, without cannon, without shoes, almost without an army, with a mere handful of men against masses, hurled himself on

---

5 Five winning numbers in a lottery.

Europe combined, and absurdly won victories in the impossible? Whence had issued that fulminating convict, who almost without taking breath, and with the same set of combatants in hand, pulverized, one after the other, the five armies of the emperor of Germany, upsetting Beaulieu on Alvinzi, Wurmser on Beaulieu, Melas on Wurmser, Mack on Melas? Who was this novice in war with the effrontery of a luminary? The academical military school excommunicated him, and as it lost its footing; hence, the implacable rancor of the old Caesarism against the new; of the regular sword against the flaming sword; and of the exchequer against genius. On the 18th of June, 1815, that rancor had the last word. and beneath Lodi, Montebello, Montenotte, Mantua, Arcola, it wrote: Waterloo. A triumph of the mediocres which is sweet to the majority. Destiny consented to this irony. In his decline, Napoleon found Wurmser, the younger, again in front of him.

In fact, to get Wurmser, it sufficed to blanch the hair of Wellington.

Waterloo is a battle of the first order, won by a captain of the second.

That which must be admired in the battle of Waterloo, is England; the English firmness, the English resolution, the English blood; the superb thing about England there, no offence to her, was herself. It was not her captain; it was her army.

Wellington, oddly ungrateful, declares in a letter to Lord Bathurst, that his army, the army which fought on the 18th of June, 1815, was a "detestable army." What does that sombre intermingling of bones buried beneath the furrows of Waterloo think of that?

England has been too modest in the matter of Wellington. To make Wellington so great is to belittle England. Wellington is nothing but a hero like many another. Those Scotch Grays, those Horse Guards, those regiments of Maitland and of Mitchell, that infantry of Pack and Kempt, that cavalry of Ponsonby and Somerset, those Highlanders playing the pibroch under the shower of grape-shot, those battalions of Rylandt, those utterly raw recruits, who hardly knew how to handle a musket holding their own against Essling's and Rivoli's old troops,--that is what was grand. Wellington was tenacious; in that lay his merit, and we are not seeking to lessen it: but the least of his foot-soldiers and of his cavalry would have been as solid as he. The iron soldier is worth as much as the Iron Duke. As for us, all our glorification goes to the English soldier, to the English army, to the English people. If trophy there be, it is to England that the trophy is due. The column of Waterloo would be more just, if, instead of the figure of a man, it bore on high the statue of a people.

But this great England will be angry at what we are saying here. She still cherishes, after her own 1688 and our 1789, the feudal illusion. She believes in heredity and hierarchy. This people, surpassed by none in power and glory, regards itself as a nation, and not as a people. And as a people, it willingly subordinates itself and takes a lord for its head. As a workman, it allows itself to be disdained; as a soldier, it allows itself to be flogged.

It will be remembered, that at the battle of Inkermann a sergeant who had, it appears, saved the army, could not be mentioned by Lord Paglan, as the English military hierarchy does not permit any hero below the grade of an officer to be mentioned in the reports.

That which we admire above all, in an encounter of the nature of Waterloo, is the marvellous cleverness of chance. A nocturnal rain, the wall of Hougomont, the hollow road of Ohain, Grouchy deaf to the cannon, Napoleon's guide deceiving him, Bulow's guide enlightening him,-- the whole of this cataclysm is wonderfully conducted.

On the whole, let us say it plainly, it was more of a massacre than of a battle at Waterloo.

Of all pitched battles, Waterloo is the one which has the smallest front for such a number of combatants. Napoleon three-quarters of a league; Wellington, half a league; seventy-two thousand combatants on each side. From this denseness the carnage arose.

The following calculation has been made, and the following proportion established: Loss of men: at Austerlitz, French, fourteen per cent; Russians, thirty per cent; Austrians, forty-four per cent. At Wagram, French, thirteen per cent; Austrians, fourteen. At the Moskowa, French, thirty-seven per cent; Russians, forty-four. At Bautzen, French, thirteen per cent; Russians and Prussians, fourteen. At Waterloo, French, fifty-six per cent; the Allies, thirty-one. Total for Waterloo, forty-one per cent; one hundred and forty-four thousand combatants; sixty thousand dead.

To-day the field of Waterloo has the calm which belongs to the earth, the impassive support of man, and it resembles all plains.

At night, moreover, a sort of visionary mist arises from it; and if a traveller strolls there, if he listens, if he watches, if he dreams like Virgil in the fatal plains of Philippi, the hallucination of the catastrophe takes possession of him. The frightful 18th of June lives again; the false monumental hillock disappears, the lion vanishes in air, the battle-field resumes its reality, lines of infantry undulate over the plain, furious gallops traverse the horizon; the frightened dreamer beholds the flash of sabres, the gleam of bayonets, the flare of bombs, the tremendous interchange of thunders; he hears, as it were, the death rattle in the depths of a tomb, the vague clamor of the battle phantom; those shadows are grenadiers, those lights are cuirassiers; that skeleton Napoleon, that other skeleton is Wellington; all this no longer exists, and yet it clashes together and combats still; and the ravines are empurpled, and the trees quiver, and there is fury even in the clouds and in the shadows; all those terrible heights, Hougomont, Mont-Saint-Jean, Frischemont, Papelotte, Plancenoit, appear confusedly crowned with whirlwinds of spectres engaged in exterminating each other.

CHAPTER XVII. IS WATERLOO TO BE CONSIDERED GOOD?

There exists a very respectable liberal school which does not hate Waterloo. We do not belong to it. To us, Waterloo is but the stupefied date of liberty. That such an eagle should emerge from such an egg is certainly unexpected.

If one places one's self at the culminating point of view of the question, Waterloo is intentionally a counter-revolutionary victory. It is Europe against France; it is Petersburg, Berlin, and Vienna against Paris; it is the statu quo against the initiative; it is the 14th of July, 1789, attacked through the 20th of March, 1815; it is the monarchies clearing the decks in opposition to the indomitable French rioting. The final extinction of that vast people which had been in eruption for twenty-six years--such was the dream. The solidarity of the Brunswicks, the Nassaus, the Romanoffs, the Hohenzollerns, the Hapsburgs with the Bourbons. Waterloo bears divine right on its crupper. It is true, that the Empire having been despotic, the kingdom by the natural reaction of things, was forced to be liberal, and that a constitutional order was the unwilling result of Waterloo, to the great regret of the conquerors. It is because revolution cannot be really conquered, and that being providential and absolutely fatal, it is always cropping up afresh: before Waterloo, in Bonaparte overthrowing the old thrones; after Waterloo, in Louis XVIII. granting and conforming to the charter. Bonaparte places a postilion on the throne of Naples, and a sergeant on the throne of Sweden, employing inequality to demonstrate equality; Louis XVIII. at Saint-Ouen countersigns the declaration of the rights of man. If you wish to gain an idea of what revolution is, call it Progress; and if you wish to acquire an idea of the nature of progress, call it To-morrow. To-morrow fulfils its work irresistibly, and it is already fulfilling it to-day. It always reaches its goal strangely. It employs Wellington to make of Foy, who was only a soldier, an orator. Foy falls at Hougomont and rises again in the tribune. Thus does progress proceed.

There is no such thing as a bad tool for that workman. It does not become disconcerted, but adjusts to its divine work the man who has bestridden the Alps, and the good old tottering invalid of Father Elysee. It makes use of the gouty man as well as of the conqueror; of the conqueror without, of the gouty man within. Waterloo, by cutting short the demolition of European thrones by the sword, had no other effect than to cause the revolutionary work to be continued in another direction. The slashers have finished; it was the turn of the thinkers. The century that Waterloo was intended to arrest has pursued its march. That sinister victory was vanquished by liberty.

In short, and incontestably, that which triumphed at Waterloo; that which smiled in Wellington's rear; that which brought him all the marshals' staffs of Europe, including, it is said, the staff of a marshal of France; that which joyously trundled the barrows full of bones to erect the knoll of the lion; that which triumphantly inscribed on that pedestal the date "June 18, 1815"; that which encouraged Blucher, as he put the flying army to the sword; that which, from the heights of the plateau of Mont-Saint-Jean, hovered over France as over its prey, was the counter-revolution. It was the counter-revolution which murmured that infamous word "dismemberment." On arriving in Paris, it beheld the crater close at hand; it felt those ashes which scorched its feet, and it changed its mind; it returned to the stammer of a charter.

Let us behold in Waterloo only that which is in Waterloo. Of intentional liberty there is none. The counter-revolution was involuntarily liberal, in the same manner as, by a corresponding phenomenon, Napoleon was involuntarily revolutionary. On the 18th of June, 1815, the mounted Robespierre was hurled from his saddle.

CHAPTER XVIII. A RECRUDESCENCE OF DIVINE RIGHT

End of the dictatorship. A whole European system crumbled away.

The Empire sank into a gloom which resembled that of the Roman world as it expired. Again we behold the abyss, as in the days of the barbarians; only the barbarism of 1815, which must be called by its pet name of the counter-revolution, was not long breathed, soon fell to panting, and halted short. The Empire was bewept,-- let us acknowledge the fact,--and bewept by heroic eyes. If glory lies in the sword converted into a sceptre, the Empire had been glory in person. It had diffused over the earth all the light which tyranny can give a sombre light. We will say more; an obscure light. Compared to the true daylight, it is night. This disappearance of night produces the effect of an eclipse.

Louis XVIII. re-entered Paris. The circling dances of the 8th of July effaced the enthusiasms of the 20th of March. The Corsican became the antithesis of the Bearnese. The flag on the dome of the Tuileries was white. The exile reigned. Hartwell's pine table took its place in front of the fleur-de-lys-strewn throne of Louis XIV. Bouvines and Fontenoy were mentioned as though they had taken place on the preceding day, Austerlitz having become antiquated. The altar and the throne fraternized majestically. One of the most undisputed forms of the health of society in the nineteenth century was established over France, and over the continent. Europe adopted the white cockade. Trestaillon was celebrated. The device non pluribus impar re-appeared on the stone rays representing a sun upon the front of the barracks on the Quai d'Orsay. Where there had been an Imperial Guard, there was now a red house. The Arc du Carrousel, all laden with badly borne victories, thrown out of its element among these novelties, a little ashamed, it may be, of Marengo and Arcola, extricated itself from its predicament with the statue of the Duc d'Angouleme. The cemetery of the Madeleine, a terrible pauper's grave in 1793, was covered with jasper and marble, since the bones of Louis XVI. and Marie Antoinette lay in that dust.

In the moat of Vincennes a sepulchral shaft sprang from the earth, recalling the fact that the Duc d'Enghien had perished in the very month when Napoleon was crowned. Pope Pius VII., who had performed the coronation very near this death, tranquilly bestowed his blessing on the fall as he had bestowed it on the elevation. At Schoenbrunn there was a little shadow, aged four, whom it was seditious to call the King of Rome. And these things took place, and the kings resumed their thrones, and the master of Europe was put in a cage, and the old regime became the new regime, and all the shadows and all the light of the earth changed place, because, on the afternoon of a certain summer's day, a shepherd said to a Prussian in the forest, "Go this way, and not that!"

This 1815 was a sort of lugubrious April. Ancient unhealthy and poisonous realities were covered with new appearances. A lie wedded 1789; the right divine was masked under a charter; fictions became constitutional; prejudices, superstitions and mental reservations, with Article 14 in the heart, were varnished over with liberalism. It was the serpent's change of skin.

Man had been rendered both greater and smaller by Napoleon. Under this reign of splendid matter, the ideal had received the strange name of ideology! It is a grave imprudence in a great man to turn the future into derision. The populace, however, that food for cannon which is so fond of the cannoneer, sought him with its glance. Where is he? What is he doing? "Napoleon is dead," said a passer-by to a veteran of Marengo and Waterloo. "He dead!" cried the soldier; "you don't know him." Imagination distrusted this man, even when overthrown.

47

The depths of Europe were full of darkness after Waterloo. Something enormous remained long empty through Napoleon's disappearance.

The kings placed themselves in this void. Ancient Europe profited by it to undertake reforms. There was a Holy Alliance; Belle-Alliance, Beautiful Alliance, the fatal field of Waterloo had said in advance.

In presence and in face of that antique Europe reconstructed, the features of a new France were sketched out. The future, which the Emperor had rallied, made its entry. On its brow it bore the star, Liberty. The glowing eyes of all young generations were turned on it. Singular fact! people were, at one and the same time, in love with the future, Liberty, and the past, Napoleon. Defeat had rendered the vanquished greater. Bonaparte fallen seemed more lofty than Napoleon erect. Those who had triumphed were alarmed. England had him guarded by Hudson Lowe, and France had him watched by Montchenu. His folded arms became a source of uneasiness to thrones. Alexander called him "my sleeplessness." This terror was the result of the quantity of revolution which was contained in him. That is what explains and excuses Bonapartist liberalism. This phantom caused the old world to tremble. The kings reigned, but ill at their ease, with the rock of Saint Helena on the horizon.

While Napoleon was passing through the death struggle at Longwood, the sixty thousand men who had fallen on the field of Waterloo were quietly rotting, and something of their peace was shed abroad over the world. The Congress of Vienna made the treaties in 1815, and Europe called this the Restoration.

This is what Waterloo was.

But what matters it to the Infinite? all that tempest, all that cloud, that war, then that peace? All that darkness did not trouble for a moment the light of that immense Eye before which a grub skipping from one blade of grass to another equals the eagle soaring from belfry to belfry on the towers of Notre Dame.

CHAPTER XIX. THE BATTLE-FIELD AT NIGHT

Let us return--it is a necessity in this book--to that fatal battle-field.

On the 18th of June the moon was full. Its light favored Blucher's ferocious pursuit, betrayed the traces of the fugitives, delivered up that disastrous mass to the eager Prussian cavalry, and aided the massacre. Such tragic favors of the night do occur sometimes during catastrophes.

After the last cannon-shot had been fired, the plain of Mont-Saint-Jean remained deserted.

The English occupied the encampment of the French; it is the usual sign of victory to sleep in the bed of the vanquished. They established their bivouac beyond Rossomme. The Prussians, let loose on the retreating rout, pushed forward. Wellington went to the village of Waterloo to draw up his report to Lord Bathurst.

If ever the sic vos non vobis was applicable, it certainly is to that village of Waterloo. Waterloo took no part, and lay half a league from the scene of action. Mont-Saint-Jean was cannonaded, Hougomont was burned, La Haie-Sainte was taken by assault, Papelotte was burned, Plancenoit was burned, La Belle-Alliance beheld the embrace of the two conquerors; these names are hardly known, and Waterloo, which worked not in the battle, bears off all the honor.

We are not of the number of those who flatter war; when the occasion presents itself, we tell the truth about it. War has frightful beauties which we have not concealed; it has also, we acknowledge, some hideous features. One of the most surprising is the prompt stripping of the bodies of the dead after the victory. The dawn which follows a battle always rises on naked corpses.

Who does this? Who thus soils the triumph? What hideous, furtive hand is that which is slipped into the pocket of victory? What pickpockets are they who ply their trade in the rear of glory? Some philosophers--Voltaire among the number--affirm that it is precisely those persons have made the glory. It is the same men, they say; there is no relief corps; those who are erect pillage those who are prone on the earth. The hero of the day is the vampire of the night. One has assuredly the right, after all, to strip a corpse a bit when one is the author of that corpse. For our own part, we do not think so; it seems to us impossible that the same hand should pluck laurels and purloin the shoes from a dead man.

One thing is certain, which is, that generally after conquerors follow thieves. But let us leave the soldier, especially the contemporary soldier, out of the question.

Every army has a rear-guard, and it is that which must be blamed. Bat-like creatures, half brigands and lackeys; all the sorts of vespertillos that that twilight called war engenders; wearers of uniforms, who take no part in the fighting; pretended invalids; formidable limpers; interloping sutlers, trotting along in little carts, sometimes accompanied by their wives, and stealing things which they sell again; beggars offering themselves as guides to officers; soldiers' servants; marauders; armies on the march in days gone by,-- we are not speaking of the present,--dragged all this behind them, so that in the special language they are called "stragglers." No army, no nation, was responsible for those beings; they spoke Italian and followed the Germans, then spoke French and followed the

English. It was by one of these wretches, a Spanish straggler who spoke French, that the Marquis of Fervacques, deceived by his Picard jargon, and taking him for one of our own men, was traitorously slain and robbed on the battle-field itself, in the course of the night which followed the victory of Cerisoles. The rascal sprang from this marauding. The detestable maxim, Live on the enemy! produced this leprosy, which a strict discipline alone could heal. There are reputations which are deceptive; one does not always know why certain generals, great in other directions, have been so popular. Turenne was adored by his soldiers because he tolerated pillage; evil permitted constitutes part of goodness. Turenne was so good that he allowed the Palatinate to be delivered over to fire and blood. The marauders in the train of an army were more or less in number, according as the chief was more or less severe. Hoche and Marceau had no stragglers; Wellington had few, and we do him the justice to mention it.

Nevertheless, on the night from the 18th to the 19th of June, the dead were robbed. Wellington was rigid; he gave orders that any one caught in the act should be shot; but rapine is tenacious. The marauders stole in one corner of the battlefield while others were being shot in another.

The moon was sinister over this plain.

Towards midnight, a man was prowling about, or rather, climbing in the direction of the hollow road of Ohain. To all appearance he was one of those whom we have just described,--neither English nor French, neither peasant nor soldier, less a man than a ghoul attracted by the scent of the dead bodies having theft for his victory, and come to rifle Waterloo. He was clad in a blouse that was something like a great coat; he was uneasy and audacious; he walked forwards and gazed behind him. Who was this man? The night probably knew more of him than the day. He had no sack, but evidently he had large pockets under his coat. From time to time he halted, scrutinized the plain around him as though to see whether he were observed, bent over abruptly, disturbed something silent and motionless on the ground, then rose and fled. His sliding motion, his attitudes, his mysterious and rapid gestures, caused him to resemble those twilight larvae which haunt ruins, and which ancient Norman legends call the Alleurs.

Certain nocturnal wading birds produce these silhouettes among the marshes.

A glance capable of piercing all that mist deeply would have perceived at some distance a sort of little sutler's wagon with a fluted wicker hood, harnessed to a famished nag which was cropping the grass across its bit as it halted, hidden, as it were, behind the hovel which adjoins the highway to Nivelles, at the angle of the road from Mont-Saint-Jean to Braine l'Alleud; and in the wagon, a sort of woman seated on coffers and packages. Perhaps there was some connection between that wagon and that prowler.

The darkness was serene. Not a cloud in the zenith. What matters it if the earth be red! the moon remains white; these are the indifferences of the sky. In the fields, branches of trees broken by grape-shot, but not fallen, upheld by their bark, swayed gently in the breeze of night. A breath, almost a respiration, moved the shrubbery. Quivers which resembled the departure of souls ran through the grass.

In the distance the coming and going of patrols and the general rounds of the English camp were audible.

Hougomont and La Haie-Sainte continued to burn, forming, one in the west, the other in the east, two great flames which were joined by the cordon of bivouac fires of the English, like a necklace of rubies with two carbuncles at the extremities, as they extended in an immense semicircle over the hills along the horizon.

We have described the catastrophe of the road of Ohain. The heart is terrified at the thought of what that death must have been to so many brave men.

If there is anything terrible, if there exists a reality which surpasses dreams, it is this: to live, to see the sun; to be in full possession of virile force; to possess health and joy; to laugh valiantly; to rush towards a glory which one sees dazzling in front of one; to feel in one's breast lungs which breathe, a heart which beats, a will which reasons; to speak, think, hope, love; to have a mother, to have a wife, to have children; to have the light--and all at once, in the space of a shout, in less than a minute, to sink into an abyss; to fall, to roll, to crush, to be crushed; to see ears of wheat, flowers, leaves, branches; not to be able to catch hold of anything; to feel one's sword useless, men beneath one, horses on top of one; to struggle in vain, since one's bones have been broken by some kick in the darkness; to feel a heel which makes one's eyes start from their sockets; to bite horses' shoes in one's rage; to stifle, to yell, to writhe; to be beneath, and to say to one's self, "But just a little while ago I was a living man!"

There, where that lamentable disaster had uttered its death-rattle, all was silence now. The edges of the hollow road were encumbered with horses and riders, inextricably heaped up. Terrible entanglement! There was no longer any slope, for the corpses had levelled the road with the plain, and reached the brim like a well-filled bushel of barley. A heap of dead bodies in the upper part, a river of blood in the lower part--such was that road on the evening of the 18th of June, 1815. The blood ran even to the Nivelles highway, and there overflowed in a large pool in front of the abatis of trees which barred the way, at a spot which is still pointed out.

It will be remembered that it was at the opposite point, in the direction of the Genappe road, that the destruction of the cuirassiers had taken place. The thickness of the layer of bodies was proportioned to the depth of the hollow road. Towards the middle, at the point where it became level, where Delort's division had passed, the layer of corpses was thinner.

The nocturnal prowler whom we have just shown to the reader was going in that direction. He was searching that vast tomb. He gazed about. He passed the dead in some sort of hideous review. He walked with his feet in the blood.

All at once he paused.

A few paces in front of him, in the hollow road, at the point where the pile of dead came to an end, an open hand, illumined by the moon, projected from beneath that heap of men. That hand had on its finger something sparkling, which was a ring of gold.

The man bent over, remained in a crouching attitude for a moment, and when he rose there was no longer a ring on the hand.

He did not precisely rise; he remained in a stooping and frightened attitude, with his back turned to the heap of dead, scanning the horizon on his knees, with the whole upper portion of his body supported on his two forefingers, which rested on the earth, and his head peering above the edge of the hollow road. The jackal's four paws suit some actions.

Then coming to a decision, he rose to his feet.

At that moment, he gave a terrible start. He felt some one clutch him from behind.

He wheeled round; it was the open hand, which had closed, and had seized the skirt of his coat.

An honest man would have been terrified; this man burst into a laugh.

"Come," said he, "it's only a dead body. I prefer a spook to a gendarme."

But the hand weakened and released him. Effort is quickly exhausted in the grave.

"Well now," said the prowler, "is that dead fellow alive? Let's see."

He bent down again, fumbled among the heap, pushed aside everything that was in his way, seized the hand, grasped the arm, freed the head, pulled out the body, and a few moments later he was dragging the lifeless, or at least the unconscious, man, through the shadows of hollow road. He was a cuirassier, an officer, and even an officer of considerable rank; a large gold epaulette peeped from beneath the cuirass; this officer no longer possessed a helmet. A furious sword-cut had scarred his face, where nothing was discernible but blood.

However, he did not appear to have any broken limbs, and, by some happy chance, if that word is permissible here, the dead had been vaulted above him in such a manner as to preserve him from being crushed. His eyes were still closed.

On his cuirass he wore the silver cross of the Legion of Honor.

The prowler tore off this cross, which disappeared into one of the gulfs which he had beneath his great coat.

Then he felt of the officer's fob, discovered a watch there, and took possession of it. Next he searched his waistcoat, found a purse and pocketed it.

When he had arrived at this stage of succor which he was administering to this dying man, the officer opened his eyes.

"Thanks," he said feebly.

The abruptness of the movements of the man who was manipulating him, the freshness of the night, the air which he could inhale freely, had roused him from his lethargy.

The prowler made no reply. He raised his head. A sound of footsteps was audible in the plain; some patrol was probably approaching.

The officer murmured, for the death agony was still in his voice:--

"Who won the battle?"

"The English," answered the prowler.

The officer went on:--

"Look in my pockets; you will find a watch and a purse. Take them."

It was already done.

The prowler executed the required feint, and said:--

"There is nothing there."

53

"I have been robbed," said the officer; "I am sorry for that. You should have had them."

The steps of the patrol became more and more distinct.

"Some one is coming," said the prowler, with the movement of a man who is taking his departure.

The officer raised his arm feebly, and detained him.

"You have saved my life. Who are you?"

The prowler answered rapidly, and in a low voice:--

"Like yourself, I belonged to the French army. I must leave you. If they were to catch me, they would shoot me. I have saved your life. Now get out of the scrape yourself."

"What is your rank?"

"Sergeant."

"What is your name?"

"Thenardier."

"I shall not forget that name," said the officer; "and do you remember mine. My name is Pontmercy."